Mastering Regulatory Changes and Compliance

Strategies for Thriving in a Dynamic Legal Landscape

Emily Lawson

© Copyright 2024 - All rights reserved.

The content contained within this book may not be reproduced, duplicated or transmitted without direct written permission from the author or the publisher.

Under no circumstances will any blame or legal responsibility be held against the publisher, or author, for any damages, reparation, or monetary loss due to the information contained within this book, either directly or indirectly.

Legal Notice:

This book is copyright protected. It is only for personal use. You cannot amend, distribute, sell, use, quote or paraphrase any part, or the content within this book, without the consent of the author or publisher.

Disclaimer Notice:

Please note the information contained within this document is for educational and entertainment purposes only. All effort has been executed to present accurate, up to date, reliable, complete information. No warranties of any kind are declared or implied. Readers acknowledge that the author is not engaging in the rendering of legal, financial, medical or professional advice. The content within this book has been derived from various sources. Please consult a licensed professional before attempting any techniques outlined in this book.

By reading this document, the reader agrees that under no circumstances is the author responsible for any losses, direct or indirect, that are incurred as a result of the use of information contained within this document, including, but not limited to, errors, omissions, or inaccuracies.

Table of Contents

INTRODUCTION

Businesses and organizations must adjust to new regulatory requirements in a constantly changing global environment. A thorough manual called "Mastering Regulatory Changes and Compliance: Strategies for Thriving in a Dynamic Legal Landscape" will assist you in navigating these challenges with assurance and forethought.

Unexpected developments in politics, the economy, technology, and social pressures can all impact regulations. Maintaining compliance for organizations involves more than just avoiding fines; it also involves developing a strong framework that can effectively anticipate and adjust to these developments. This book explores the core of regulatory settings, including information on significant regulatory organizations, historical trends, and the effects of globalization on compliance.

We'll look at all the important parts of a strong compliance program, like risk analysis, policy creation, and cutting-edge technology integration. We'll look closely at industry-specific legislation and offer useful tips for industries including healthcare, banking, and environmental management. This guide will also provide proactive ways to react to regulatory changes so that your compliance tactics are resilient, forward-thinking, and reactive.

Navigating this terrain also requires careful consideration of ethical and legal issues. Sustainable compliance procedures revolve around balancing company goals and moral and legal commitments. By the time you finish reading this book, you'll know exactly how to future-proof your compliance programs and create a compliance culture that is creative, flexible, and resilient to change.

CHAPTER I

Understanding the Regulatory Environment

Historical Perspective on Regulatory Changes

Comprehending today's regulatory landscape and projecting future developments requires understanding the historical perspective on regulation changes. As society has evolved, regulations have changed due to social movements, political and economic agendas, and technological breakthroughs. This section examines the beginnings and development of regulatory frameworks, emphasizing significant turning points and their effects on current compliance procedures.

Regulations were first created by the rulers of ancient civilizations to preserve law and order and to safeguard the interests of the state. One of the oldest known legal codes from ancient Mesopotamia, the Code of Hammurabi, contained rules for commerce, property rights, and civil behavior. Similarly, many contemporary legal doctrines have their roots in the legal framework of ancient Rome, namely in the Corpus Juris Civilis. Upholding social order and promoting economic exchanges were the fundamental goals of these early legislation.

The development of nation-states during the medieval and early modern eras brought about a profound change in governmental procedures. Regulations were first put in place by monarchies and newly formed governments to regulate economic activity, especially trade and commerce. This approach was typified by the mercantilist policies of the 16th and 17th centuries when governments regulated imports, exports, and colonial trade to increase national wealth. These rules aimed to safeguard homegrown businesses and optimize the gain of valuable metals.

New regulatory frameworks were required due to the significant changes in economic and social structures brought about by the Industrial Revolution in the 18th and 19th centuries. Fast industrialization brought about major changes in labor dynamics, urbanization, and the growth of factory systems. These modifications brought attention to the necessity of legislation covering public health, work conditions, and environmental effects. Beginning in 1802, the Factory Acts in the United Kingdom were one of the first major regulatory reactions to industrialization to enhance factory working conditions, especially for women and children.

The late 19th and early 20th centuries' Progressive Era was crucial in creating contemporary regulatory systems. Governments in the US and Europe enacted several reforms to limit corporate excesses and safeguard public welfare in response to the social and economic issues brought on by rapid industrialization. This tendency was demonstrated by founding regulatory organizations like the Federal Trade Commission (FTC) in 1914 and the Interstate Commerce Commission (ICC) in 1887 in the

United States. These organizations were in charge of upholding laws about consumer protection, monopolies, and commercial practices.

The 1930s Great Depression highlighted how robust regulatory frameworks were necessary to safeguard citizens and stable economies. Several regulatory changes were implemented in the US under President Franklin D. Roosevelt's New Deal to revive the economy and avoid further financial crises. In direct reaction to the 1929 stock market crisis, the Securities and Exchange Commission (SEC) was founded in 1934 to oversee the securities sector and safeguard investors. Comparably, a larger tendency toward social welfare regulation was reflected in the 1935 establishment of the Social Security Administration (SSA), which sought financial security for the unemployed and old.

Following World War II, regulatory frameworks grew to meet new difficulties brought about by globalization and technical breakthroughs. For example, the International Atomic Energy Agency (IAEA) was established in 1957 to promote safe and peaceful uses of nuclear energy due to the fast development of nuclear technology. Similarly, the emergence of multinational companies and international commerce required the creation of global regulatory frameworks, as demonstrated by the founding of the World Commerce Organization (WTO) in 1995 and the General Agreement on Tariffs and Trade (GATT) in 1947.

As worries about pollution and resource depletion grew, environmental regulations became more prevalent in the second half of the 20th century. The United States took a major stride toward comprehensive ecological control by creating the Environmental Protection Agency (EPA) and other landmark laws like the Clean Air Act of 1970. These legislative frameworks, which addressed hazardous waste management, air and water pollution, and resource preservation, reflected a larger social movement favoring environmental sustainability.

The late 20th and early 21st centuries saw the emergence of the digital age, which brought new regulatory difficulties and required the creation of innovative regulatory frameworks. New regulatory sectors like data protection, cybersecurity, and digital commerce have emerged due to the transformation of economic and social relations brought about by the rise of the internet and digital technology. In 2018, the European Union enacted the General Data Protection Regulation (GDPR), a major regulatory response to digitalization issues that aim to safeguard people's data and privacy in an increasingly interconnected world.

Recent decades have seen a rise in the significance of social and ethical regulatory frameworks and technology breakthroughs. The emergence of social movements that support racial justice, gender equality, and corporate responsibility has led to the creation of laws that support inclusion, diversity, and equity. Social responsibility integration into legislative frameworks is shown in establishing diversity quotas and corporate governance legislation in different nations.

The COVID-19 pandemic has brought attention to the need for regulatory frameworks to maintain economic stability and manage public health emergencies. To meet the issues posed by the epidemic, governments across the globe have implemented a variety of regulatory measures, ranging from financial relief programs and economic stimulus packages to public health guidelines and vaccine distribution methods. These regulatory reactions highlight the need for flexible and strong regulatory structures to handle unseen difficulties.

The historical perspective on regulatory developments offers important insights into the dynamic character of regulation and the forces shaping its evolution as we look to the future. Regulatory frameworks will continue to be shaped by the dynamic interaction of political, economic, technological, and social forces, requiring constant innovation and adaptation. To successfully navigate this complicated regulatory environment, businesses and organizations must be watchful and proactive, using historical data to predict emerging patterns and create effective compliance plans.

To sum up, the historical viewpoint on regulatory changes emphasizes how frameworks for regulations are always changing to meet the demands of a changing society. From antiquated legal codes to contemporary regulatory bodies, the need to uphold social order, safeguard the public interest, and foster economic stability has shaped the evolution of regulations. Understanding the historical background of regulatory developments lays the groundwork for creating innovative and successful compliance methods as we traverse the complexity of the modern regulatory landscape. We can ensure that our regulatory frameworks continue to be flexible, resilient, and in line with societal values and goals by using the lessons we've learned from the past to predict better and address the regulatory difficulties of the future.

Key Regulatory Bodies and Their Roles

Regulatory agencies are essential to preserving different industries' integrity, equity, and stability. They create guidelines, monitor adherence, and impose penalties to safeguard the public and ensure companies follow the law. This section examines important industry regulatory organizations and how they have shaped the regulatory environment.

The Securities and Exchange Commission (SEC) is one of the most powerful regulatory agencies in the US. The SEC was created in 1934 to react to the 1929 stock market disaster to safeguard investors, preserve honest and efficient markets, and promote capital formation. The SEC manages securities exchanges, enforces federal securities laws, and controls the securities sector. It guarantees transparency and aids investors' decision-making by requiring public corporations to report financial information. The SEC keeps an eye out for and looks into insider trading, securities fraud, and other infractions that compromise the integrity of the financial markets.

The Food and Drug Administration (FDA) regulates the efficacy and safety of medications, food, cosmetics, and medical equipment in the US and is another essential regulatory agency. The FDA was founded in 1906 to safeguard the general public's health by assuring these products' efficacy, security, and safety. Before new medications and medical equipment are approved for sale, the FDA performs inspections, examines clinical trials, and assesses their efficacy and safety. It also controls tobacco products' production, promotion, and distribution to safeguard the public's health. Regarding food safety, the FDA is involved in standard-setting, inspections, and recalls of tainted or mislabeled food items.

The Federal Reserve, or the Fed, is a crucial regulatory organization in the financial industry. The Federal Reserve, the nation's central bank, was founded in 1913 and is responsible for developing and carrying out monetary policy. Its main goals are maximizing employment, maintaining price stability, and maintaining reasonable long-term interest rates. The Fed oversees and regulates banks to guarantee the stability and safety of the country's banking and financial system. Additionally, it offers financial services to foreign official entities, the US government, and depository institutions. The Federal Reserve controls the nation's money supply and interest rates and contributes to preserving economic stability.

Another important regulatory agency entrusted with safeguarding the environment and public health is the Environmental Protection Agency (EPA). The EPA was founded in 1970 and is responsible for creating and enforcing regulations about hazardous waste management, chemical safety, and air and water pollution. In addition to researching and establishing environmental standards, the agency also uses enforcement actions and inspections to guarantee compliance. The EPA's responsibilities include promoting sustainable practices, safeguarding natural resources, and supervising the cleaning of hazardous areas. The EPA seeks to protect human health and lessen the negative effects of industrial activity on the environment by regulating pollutants and establishing emission limits.

The Federal Communications Commission (FCC) is a key regulatory body in the telecommunications industry. The Federal Communications Commission (FCC) was founded in 1934 and oversees interstate and worldwide communications in the US via wire, satellite, cable, and television. The FCC was established to safeguard the security, dependability, and accessibility of communications networks while encouraging competition, innovation, and investment in broadband services. The FCC sets aside spectrum for various purposes, including wireless communications and broadcasting, and it also imposes rules to keep interference at bay and guarantee effective spectrum utilization. It manages broadcast content regulation, licenses radio, and television stations, and supports universal service to ensure all Americans can access telecommunications services.

The International Atomic Energy Agency (IAEA) is a major nuclear energy regulatory organization on a global scale. The IAEA was founded in 1957 with the goals of preventing the proliferation of atomic weapons and advancing the peaceful use of nuclear energy. The agency encourages sharing scientific and technical information and offers a framework for international collaboration in the peaceful use of nuclear technology. The IAEA helps member states improve their nuclear safety and security regimes and performs inspections to ensure that nuclear materials are not diverted to weapons projects. The IAEA advances international peace and security by encouraging nuclear technology's safe and secure application.

The global commerce system is supervised by the World Trade Organization (WTO), another significant international regulatory organization. The World Trade Organization (WTO), founded in 1995, offers a platform for trade agreement negotiations, dispute resolution, and policy implementation oversight. Ensuring smooth, predictable, and unhindered international trade is its main objective. WTO agreements and regulations safeguard intellectual property rights, encourage fair competition, and lower trade barriers. The World Trade Organization contributes to the stability and predictability of the international trading system by offering a forum for trade discussions and dispute settlement.

The World Health Organization (WHO) is a vital global regulatory body in the healthcare industry. The WHO was founded in 1948 to promote health, ensure international security, and aid the weak. The WHO coordinates national responses to public health emergencies, establishes worldwide health standards, and offers technical aid to nations. It carries out studies, creates guidelines, and promotes laws enhancing health outcomes. The WHO addresses non-communicable diseases, encourages immunization, and controls infectious diseases. The World Health Organization (WHO) is crucial to strengthening global health since it leads and organizes worldwide health initiatives.

An intergovernmental body called the Financial Action Task Force (FATF) was founded in 1989 to address challenges to the integrity of the global financial system, including money laundering and the funding of terrorism. The FATF creates and advocates policies that guard against abuse of the international monetary system. It ensures that member nations implement efficient measures to combat financial crimes by conducting peer reviews and setting global standards. The FATF's recommendations are accepted as the industry norm for initiatives aimed at preventing money laundering and countering the funding of terrorism. The FATF improves the integrity and stability of the international financial system by encouraging the efficient use of these standards.

In summary, regulatory agencies are critical to preserving different industries' integrity, equity, and stability. These agencies, which range from the US government's SEC and FDA to global institutions like the WHO, WTO, and IAEA, set guidelines, enforce them and monitor compliance to safeguard the public and ensure companies follow the law. Their job includes everything from environmental preservation and trade monitoring to financial regulation and public health. Navigating the complex regulatory landscape and guaranteeing compliance in a dynamic and interconnected world requires an understanding of the roles played by these regulatory organizations.

The Impact of Globalization on Regulatory Compliance

The globe has changed significantly due to globalization, merging economies, cultures, and legal frameworks. Global trade, investment, and communication networks are expanding at a rapid pace, which has brought forth both extraordinary potential and difficult hurdles for organizations, especially when it comes to regulatory compliance. To better understand how globalization affects regulatory compliance, this section will examine how regulations are convergent, how multinational regulatory frameworks are growing, what obstacles multinational corporations face, and how they navigate this complicated environment.

Global market integration requires some level of regulatory convergence. Businesses that operate internationally face a variety of regulatory regimes, some of which differ greatly from one government to the next. This variability may cause disagreements and complicate compliance. A drive has been made to harmonize rules to build a more unified global regulatory framework to address these problems. Organizations like the World Trade Organization (WTO) and the International Organization for Standardization (ISO) are critical in encouraging regulatory convergence by creating international standards and facilitating agreements that harmonize regulatory norms. Uniform laws ease the burden on global corporations, allowing them to optimize their processes and guarantee adherence to various legal frameworks.

Regulatory convergence is sometimes complicated, though. International standards can offer a common framework, but local laws frequently take into account particular political, economic, and cultural settings. For example, there are significant differences in data protection laws between the sector-specific approach in the US and the General Data Protection Regulation (GDPR) of the European Union. Global businesses may face serious compliance issues as a result of these disparities. Companies must manage disorganized rules to ensure their operations respect worldwide standards and local legislation. This necessitates a thorough comprehension of local regulatory environments and the capacity to modify compliance plans.

Another noteworthy effect of globalization on regulatory compliance is the emergence of transnational regulatory frameworks. National rules are influenced by guidelines and frameworks established by organizations like the Basel Committee on Banking Supervision (BCBS), the International Monetary Fund (IMF), and the Financial Action Task Force (FATF). For example, the Financial Action Task Force (FATF) establishes global guidelines to prevent money laundering and terrorist financing, which member nations enact into national laws. Similarly, the Basel Accords offer a legal framework for banking oversight, fostering international financial stability. These international frameworks improve global economic stability by lowering regulatory arbitrage and promoting a more uniform regulatory environment.

The globalization of regulatory compliance poses significant hurdles for organizations, notwithstanding these efforts. The complexity of handling compliance across several jurisdictions is one of the main obstacles. The regulatory environment that multinational firms operate in is complex, with wide variations in terms of its scope, enforcement, and interpretation. Governments constantly update and modify their legal frameworks to address new dangers and issues, which adds to the complexity of regulations. It takes substantial resources and experience to stay on top of these changes and guarantee compliance in various regulatory contexts.

Potential problems with regulations present another difficulty. Businesses that operate internationally may encounter compliance problems due to competing regulatory requirements. For instance, a company operating in the EU and the US could have to comply with various data protection laws, making data management more difficult. To resolve these disputes, one must carefully weigh legal and strategic options and communicate effectively with regulatory bodies to negotiate compliance routes and obtain clarifications.

Additionally, the possibility of regulatory enforcement measures is increased by globalization. Businesses that grow internationally fall under the attention of several regulatory agencies. This raises the possibility of encountering enforcement actions for non-compliance, which can lead to hefty fines, harm to one's reputation, and interruptions to operations. In a globalized setting, high-profile incidents like the Volkswagen emissions scandal and the Facebook-Cambridge Analytica data leak highlight the serious consequences of regulatory non-compliance. Businesses must invest significantly in compliance procedures to track and manage regulatory risks throughout their international operations.

Businesses are implementing various tactics to improve regulatory compliance in a globalized setting in response to these problems. The establishment of thorough compliance management systems is one such tactic. Centralized monitoring and control are made possible by these systems, which integrate compliance procedures throughout the company. Cutting-edge technologies like blockchain, AI, and machine learning are increasingly used to improve data accuracy, automate repetitive compliance operations, and improve compliance monitoring. Businesses can enhance their capacity to identify and address compliance risks quickly by implementing these solutions.

Building an organizational culture of compliance is another essential tactic. Compliance needs to be ingrained in the organization's operations and principles; it cannot be the exclusive domain of the legal or compliance departments. This includes educating staff members about compliance standards, supporting moral conduct, and pushing for early detection and resolution of compliance issues. Employee commitment to upholding regulatory standards in their everyday activities and understanding of the necessity of compliance are both enhanced by a strong compliance culture.

Cooperation with regulatory bodies is also essential for efficient compliance in a globalized world. Businesses should interact with authorities to ask for advice, elucidate specifications, and openly disclose compliance problems. Having a good rapport with regulatory agencies can help to promote cooperative communication and cooperation, which lowers the possibility of enforcement actions and allows compliance concerns to be resolved more successfully. Companies can also join forums and associations in their industry to learn about new regulations and network with companies with similar practices.

The growth of external experts and compliance consulting organizations who specialize in negotiating complex regulatory landscapes is another effect of globalization. These businesses provide invaluable information and experience to assist companies in managing compliance across several jurisdictions. Companies can lower the risk of non-compliance and improve their compliance capabilities by utilizing the skills and knowledge of outside consultants.

In conclusion, globalization has substantially impacted regulatory compliance because globalization has led to regulatory convergence, increased regulatory environment complexity, and the emergence of transnational regulatory frameworks. These advancements provide significant hurdles for firms, even as they present chances for improved global stability and efficient operations. Strategic planning, substantial resources, and regulatory knowledge are needed to manage compliance across jurisdictions, resolve regulatory issues, and reduce enforcement risks. Businesses can successfully manage the challenges of international regulatory compliance by implementing thorough compliance management systems, encouraging a compliance culture, working with regulatory bodies, and utilizing outside expertise. Businesses must be alert and flexible as globalization develops to ensure their compliance procedures are strong, resilient, and equipped to handle the ever-changing regulatory demands of a globalized world.

Case Studies of Major Regulatory Changes

Regulation changes can significantly affect several industries, from consumer behavior to market dynamics. Analyzing case studies of important regulatory changes provides an understanding of how these changes influence societal outcomes and economic environments. The deregulation of the US airline industry, the implementation of the General Data Protection Regulation (GDPR) in the EU, and the revision of financial regulations in the wake of the 2008 financial crisis are three prominent instances that highlight the extensive consequences of regulatory reform.

In the history of regulations, the deregulation of the airline sector in the United States in 1978 was a significant event. Before deregulation, the Civil Aeronautics Board (CAB) controlled routes, fares, and timetables, resulting in little competition and high costs. The objectives of the 1978 Airline Deregulation Act were to promote competition, lower costs, and give customers more options. This modification in the law gave airlines the freedom to choose their schedules and rates, greatly impacting the sector. Fares decreased, and the number of passengers increased immediately, demonstrating the beneficial effect on consumer access to air travel. Deregulation brought about certain difficulties, including market consolidation and financial instability for certain carriers. As low-cost airlines and more competitive international routes emerged, the sector saw increased efficiency and innovation. The aviation industry's deregulation exemplifies how, despite some trade-offs, doing away with regulatory restrictions may increase competition and benefit customers.

The General Data Protection Regulation (GDPR), implemented in the European Union in 2018, brought about a major change in global data privacy regulations. The GDPR was created to offer people more control over their data and to standardize data protection rules among EU member states. Businesses were subject to strict guidelines for gathering, storing, and processing data, and non-compliance had harsh consequences. The GDPR had an instantaneous and broad effect. Enterprises were required to restructure their procedures for managing data, establish fresh privacy guidelines, and guarantee strong data protection protocols. Small and medium-sized firms (SMEs) faced substantial compliance issues with the rule despite its intended protection of consumer rights and privacy enhancement. Despite these obstacles, the GDPR has established a global benchmark for data protection, impacting privacy laws in other jurisdictions. The GDPR framework inspires regulations such as the California Consumer Privacy Act (CCPA) and other comparable legislation. The regulation has sparked a wider discussion over consumer rights and data ethics in the digital era.

Regulations in the financial sector were changed in reaction to the 2008 financial crisis to mitigate the systemic risks that caused the collapse. One of the biggest revisions to financial regulation since the Great Depression was made in the United States in 2010 with the passage of the Dodd-Frank Wall Street Reform and Consumer Protection Act. The act aimed to lower risk, boost transparency, and avert more financial catastrophes. Important measures included the establishment of the Consumer Financial Protection Bureau (CFPB), more stringent bank capital requirements, and the Volcker Rule, which restricted commercial banks' ability to engage in proprietary trading. The Dodd-Frank Act greatly impacted the financial industry, which resulted in notable modifications to how financial institutions function. Some claim that the more stringent oversight and compliance requirements it imposed stunted growth and innovation. Supporters assert, however, that the legislation has strengthened the financial system's resilience and reduced its susceptibility to the kind of careless activity that caused the crisis. The act also highlighted the difficulties in managing systemic risk in an international economy by igniting discussions about balancing market freedom and regulation.

The United States' 2010 enactment of the Affordable Care Act (ACA) brought another major regulatory reform. The goals of the ACA were to lower healthcare costs, boost the number of people with health insurance, and enhance patient outcomes. The creation of health insurance exchanges, the extension of Medicaid, and the introduction of laws mandating that people carry insurance and that employers supply it were among the important provisions. The Affordable Care Act (ACA) significantly changed the healthcare environment by expanding the number of Americans with health insurance and implementing cost-control measures. But it also encountered strong legal challenges and political resistance, underscoring the divisive character of healthcare reform. The ACA's ongoing effects on customers, insurance markets, and the healthcare sector show the long-term effects of significant regulatory changes.

Another crucial example of a regulatory reform is the banking industry's adoption of the Basel III requirements. Basel III tightened capital and liquidity rules for banks to improve their resilience to financial shocks in response to the shortcomings exposed by the 2008 financial crisis. These laws were designed to lessen the probability of bank collapses and shield the whole economy from systemic threats. Basel III reduced leverage and increased global financial stability by requiring banks to retain high-quality capital and maintain stronger liquidity coverage. The international banking sector has been greatly impacted by Basel III's adoption, which has led banks to fortify their balance sheets and embrace more stringent risk management procedures. Supporters of the measures contend that they are required to guarantee a more stable and resilient financial sector, despite some critics' claims that the additional regulatory burden could limit lending and economic growth.

The United States' introduction of the Clean Air Act Amendments of 1990 is a key case study in environmental control. The purpose of these revisions was to address emissions of toxic air, urban air pollution, and acid rain. The creation of a sulfur dioxide (SO_2) emission cap and trade program, which attempted to lessen acid rain, was one of the historic clauses. Companies could purchase and sell emission permits thanks to this market-based strategy, which offered financial incentives for lowering pollution. The cap-and-trade scheme demonstrated market-based regulatory methods' efficacy, effectively decreasing SO_2 emissions. The United States air quality has been significantly improved, and public health has improved due to the Clean Air Act Amendments of 1990, which also considerably reduced dangerous pollution.

These case studies of significant regulatory changes demonstrate the complexity and breadth of the implications of regulatory reform. Regulatory reforms can transform industries, affect economic behavior, and impact societal results. These changes can be directed towards restoring competition, defending consumer rights, guaranteeing financial stability, increasing healthcare coverage, or protecting the environment. These instances highlight how crucial it is to properly plan and execute regulations to balance the advantages of supervision and protection and any potential drawbacks or difficulties. Regulation's role will be essential in managing the complexity of today's economy and tackling new issues as societies change.

Future Trends in Regulatory Environments

Investigating forthcoming regulatory framework changes is imperative to comprehend how marketplaces and industries will adjust to novel obstacles and prospects. The growing use of technology in regulatory procedures is one such development. The emergence of RegTech, or regulatory technology, is changing the way that compliance is kept track of and implemented. This section involves using blockchain, AI, and machine learning to improve transparency, expedite regulatory reporting, and lower the possibility of human error. Because of these technologies, real-time monitoring and analysis are possible, facilitating regulators' ability to identify and address compliance issues quickly. To detect trends and anomalies that can point to fraud or non-compliance, machine learning algorithms, for example, can examine huge datasets. This increases the efficacy and efficiency of regulatory supervision.

The increased focus on environmental standards and sustainability is another significant development. Governments and regulatory agencies are implementing stricter laws to encourage sustainable behavior as ecological degradation and climate change become more widely recognized issues. This includes laws to lower carbon emissions, support renewable energy sources, and advance corporate social responsibility. Businesses must now implement more ecologically friendly procedures; non-compliance can result in costly fines and harm to their brand. Businesses are compelled to innovate and invest in green technologies by the European Union's Green Deal, which aims to reduce greenhouse gas emissions and increase energy efficiency through aggressive targets.

Data privacy and cybersecurity are becoming increasingly important, changing the regulatory landscape. Regulatory agencies enforce stricter data protection standards due to increasing data breaches and cyberattacks. Similar laws are being introduced in other places. The General Data Protection Regulation (GDPR) in Europe established a precedent for data privacy legislation globally. These laws mandate that businesses have strong cybersecurity safeguards, handle personal data securely, and have transparent procedures for notifying customers of data breaches. It is anticipated that authorities will continue to update and broaden their standards to handle new dangers, putting even more emphasis on data privacy. For example, the US's California Consumer Privacy Act (CCPA) has given customers increased privacy rights and influenced state law.

The regulatory landscape is also growing increasingly international. Businesses operating internationally and participating in global trade are making international cooperation and regulatory harmonization more and more crucial. To promote global company operations and avoid regulatory arbitrage, groups like the International Organization of Securities Commissions (IOSCO) and the Financial Action Task Force (FATF) strive to establish uniform regulatory standards. This tendency is especially noticeable when it comes to financial rules since maintaining the integrity and stability of financial markets requires international cooperation. For instance, the Basel III framework seeks to improve global banking industry regulation, oversight, and risk management.

Regulations in the healthcare industry are changing in tandem with advancements in drugs and medical technology. Due to regulators implementing flexible regulatory frameworks and expedited review schedules, new pharmaceuticals and medical devices are being approved through more efficient and streamlined processes. This approach aims to protect patient safety while hastening the availability of novel treatments. In addition, the field of personalized medicine is gaining popularity, necessitating the development of new regulatory strategies to handle the complexity of customized care. For example, the Food and Drug Administration (FDA) in the United States has launched programs to encourage the creation and authorization of precision medicines, which customize medical interventions based on a patient's unique genetic makeup.

The growing participation of stakeholders in the regulatory process is another significant trend. To ensure policies are fair and successful, regulators request more feedback from the public, consumer advocacy organizations, and industry experts. By addressing the needs and concerns of all stakeholders, more inclusive and transparent regulatory frameworks are produced with the aid of this participatory method. Public consultations, stakeholder gatherings, and cooperative working groups are increasingly standard procedures in the regulatory process. Environmental regulations are a good example of this trend, as they frequently seek public input to create policies on air pollution, water quality, and land use.

Geopolitical and economic issues also influence future developments in regulation. For example, changes in political power, trade conflicts, and financial penalties affect the enforcement and priority of rules. Regulators must adjust to these changes to keep the market stable and equitable. The increasing digitization of society and the emergence of virtual currencies, like cryptocurrencies, are forcing authorities to create new frameworks to deal with the particular problems these technologies provide. As an illustration, regulatory frameworks are being built to control central bank digital currencies (CBDCs) issuance and use.

Furthermore, ethical issues are receiving more and more attention in the regulatory framework. Regulations are paying more attention to topics like genetic engineering, artificial intelligence ethics, and the moral implications of emerging technology. Authorities strive to create policies and norms that guarantee moral behavior in developing and applying cutting-edge technologies. This pattern reflects a larger social anxiety over how technology affects privacy, human rights, and moral principles. To address the ethical concerns of AI, for example, the European Commission's proposal for AI regulation includes clauses that guarantee AI systems' responsibility, transparency, and fairness.

Modifying regulatory frameworks to consider the gig economy and shifting labor markets is another new trend. Traditional labor laws are being reassessed to preserve workers' rights and guarantee decent working conditions as more people take on temporary, freelance, or part-time employment. This covers laws about benefits, job security, and the minimum wage. Legislators are discussing how to categorize gig workers and their rights, which indicates the need to update labor laws in light of changing employment trends in many nations.

Moreover, there is a growing trend in incorporating social justice and equality principles into regulatory frameworks. Regulators are paying more attention to ensuring everyone has equal access to opportunities and resources and that laws do not disproportionately affect vulnerable communities. Policies that address systemic inequality and encourage diversity are being developed in several sectors, including housing, healthcare, and education.

In summary, technological integration, sustainability, data privacy, globalization, healthcare innovation, stakeholder involvement, economic and geopolitical influences, ethical considerations, labor market adaptations, and social justice initiatives are characteristics of future trends in regulatory environments. These patterns demonstrate the dynamic regulatory environments and how constant adaptation is required to take advantage of fresh opportunities and difficulties. Organizations must be proactive and knowledgeable to manage these changing regulatory environments successfully. Businesses can better position themselves to comply with rules, reduce risks, and seize new possibilities in a world that is changing quickly by understanding and anticipating these trends.

CHAPTER II

Building a Compliance Framework

Components of an Effective Compliance Program

Any firm must have an efficient compliance program to guarantee compliance with laws, regulations, and internal procedures. Strong leadership and dedication from the top are the cornerstones of any successful compliance program. The board of directors and top management must actively support and openly embrace the compliance program to establish a culture that stresses the value of moral behavior and compliance across the company. A top-down approach is crucial in cultivating a compliance culture since employees are inclined to emulate their leaders' prioritization of these values.

Another essential element is risk assessment. An organization's specific operations, industry, and regulatory environment risks must be identified, evaluated, and prioritized. This entails carefully examining all possible compliance risks, including those related to finances, operations, law, and reputation. By being aware of these risks, the company can focus its compliance efforts on the most important areas and ensure resources are used efficiently to reduce possible problems.

Policies and procedures must be thorough and unambiguous to guide staff members on compliance-related issues. These documents must be well written, easily available, and updated often to consider modifications to the business's legislation, rules, and procedures. Important topics include data protection, conflict of interest, anti-corruption, and reporting procedures for alleged wrongdoing should be included. Employees who are well-versed in policies and procedures know exactly what is expected of them and how to manage circumstances about compliance.

Education and training are essential components of a successful compliance program. Workers at all levels need frequent training on the organization's ethical standards, regulations, and procedures for compliance. Training curricula must be interesting, pertinent, and customized to staff members' roles and duties. Frequent training guarantees that staff members are aware of their responsibilities regarding compliance and comprehend the possible repercussions of non-adherence. Moreover, continuing education contributes to reaffirming the significance of conformity and moral conduct as essential components of the corporate culture.

Monitoring and audits are essential to guarantee the compliance program's efficacy. Frequent monitoring procedures, such as compliance reviews and internal audits, assist in identifying and resolving possible compliance problems before they become more serious. To ensure objectivity, unbiased, independent individuals should carry out these tasks. Senior management and the board should receive recorded reports detailing the results of monitoring and auditing efforts, together with suggestions for remedial measures. By keeping an eye on things, the company may spot patterns, gauge how well the compliance program works, and make the required corrections to deal with new threats.

A strong communication and reporting framework is essential to a successful compliance program. Workers need to be able to report suspected misbehavior or compliance infractions without worrying about facing consequences. Establishing private and easily available reporting channels, like hotlines or online reporting platforms, is necessary. The company must also ensure that staff members are informed of the reporting options and stress the value of reporting. Employees are encouraged to voice concerns when management communicates clearly about the company's non-retaliation rules.

The application of rules and discipline is another essential element. It is imperative for the business to maintain a consistent enforcement of its compliance standards and to impose suitable disciplinary measures on those who fail to comply. This discourages wrongdoing in the future and shows the organization's dedication to maintaining its standards. Discipline policies should be reasonable, uniform, and commensurate with the seriousness of the infraction. Recognizing and rewarding staff members who exhibit excellent compliance behavior is another important part of effective enforcement, as it serves to highlight the advantages of upholding policies and moral principles.

A successful compliance program has ongoing improvement tools as well. This entails regularly evaluating and revising the program to consider modifications to industry practices, organizational risks, and regulatory environments. Maintaining the compliance program's relevance and efficacy in tackling present and upcoming issues is ensured by ongoing improvement. To make informed changes to policies, processes, and training programs, consideration should be given to employee feedback, audit findings, and lessons learned from previous compliance difficulties.

Another crucial element is how compliance is incorporated into the company governance structure. Instead of being seen as an independent job, compliance should be seen as a critical component of the organization's risk management and governance procedures. Through this integration, organizational culture, operational procedures, and strategic decision-making are guaranteed to incorporate compliance considerations. To coordinate activities and exchange information, the compliance function should collaborate closely with other departments like legal, finance, and human resources.

Another essential element of a successful compliance program is third-party management. Businesses frequently collaborate with various other parties, including suppliers, contractors, and business partners, which raises the possibility of extra compliance issues. Due diligence is one aspect of a thorough third-party management process, monitoring third-party operations and ensuring they follow the organization's compliance guidelines. Contracts involving third parties must contain explicit requirements for compliance and procedures for handling non-compliance.

Finally, sufficient funding and assistance are needed for compliance initiatives to be successful. This entails assigning adequate funds, workforce, and technology resources to carry out and uphold the compliance program. The compliance function needs direct access to top management and the board and the ability and independence to make decisions to function well. Investing in the required resources gives the business the infrastructure to sustain a strong program and shows its commitment to compliance.

Finally, commitment from the leadership, risk assessment, well-defined policies and procedures, education and training, monitoring and auditing, reporting and communication systems, discipline and enforcement, ongoing improvement, integration with corporate governance, third-party management, and sufficient resources are all essential elements of a successful compliance program. Together, these components provide a thorough and dynamic compliance program that identifies and prevents infractions and fosters an ethical and accountable culture within the company. Organizations may negotiate complex regulatory environments, reduce risks, and establish a solid basis for long-term success by successfully adopting these components.

Risk Assessment and Management

Organizations use risk assessment and management as essential procedures to find, assess, and reduce possible risks that could hurt their business operations, financial results, and reputation. Finding the hazards a business may encounter is the first stage in the risk assessment process. This calls for a thorough examination of both internal and external influences. Organizational structure, procedures, and employee conduct are examples of internal influences; economic situations, legislative changes, technology developments, and competitive dynamics are external elements. By comprehensively comprehending these variables, entities can establish an elaborate list of possible hazards.

Assessing a risk's likelihood and potential impact comes next after it has been discovered. Both qualitative and quantitative analysis are used in this evaluation. Expert opinion and scenario analysis, which looks at several possible future scenarios and their effects on the business, are also included in qualitative analysis. On the other hand, quantitative analysis estimates the likelihood and potential financial impact of hazards discovered using statistical techniques and historical data. By taking a dual approach, companies can thoroughly understand risks and rank them according to their likelihood and severity.

Organizations analyze risks and then create management plans for them. Four broad categories can be used to classify risk management strategies: acceptance, transfer, reduction, and avoidance. Taking steps to eliminate danger, usually by stopping the activities that cause it, is risk avoidance. The main goal of risk reduction is implementing strategies to lessen a risk's impact or possibility. To avoid future problems, this can entail investing in technology, streamlining operating procedures, or strengthening security measures. Transferring risk to a different party entails doing so, usually by outsourcing specific tasks or obtaining insurance. When a company chooses to accept a risk and its possible consequences, it usually does so because the expense of risk reduction outweighs the possibility of loss.

Internal control implementation is a crucial component of risk management. These controls are guidelines and practices to stop or identify mistakes, fraud, and other anomalies. Segregation of duties, which divides important tasks among multiple employees to prevent fraud; authorization controls, which guarantee that all transactions are approved by designated personnel; and reconciliation processes, which compare financial records with actual data regularly to spot discrepancies, are examples of effective internal controls. Establishing strong internal controls can help firms drastically lower the risks they face.

Important elements of the risk management process include risk monitoring and review. This entails keeping a close eye on the risk environment and the efficiency of risk management techniques. Audits and assessments are carried out regularly to ensure that controls are operating as intended and to spot any new or developing risks. Organizations should also set up key risk indicators (KRIs), which offer early warning indicators of possible problems. KRIs are metrics that monitor information linked to risk, such as the frequency of security lapses or shifts in the state of the market. Organizations can proactively manage hazards before they escalate by monitoring these indications.

A strong risk culture is also necessary for effective organizational risk management. This indicates that workers at all levels recognize the value of risk management and are motivated to recognize and disclose possible hazards. Setting the example at the top and exhibiting a dedication to risk management are two important ways leadership contributes to developing this culture. Maintaining this culture and ensuring that staff members are prepared to support the company's risk management initiatives are made possible by regular training and communication regarding risk policies and procedures.

Risk management and assessment are continual processes that must be adjusted to new situations rather than one-time events. The risk landscape is ever-changing, with new threats appearing as markets, technology, and legal frameworks change. Companies must update their risk assessments regularly and modify their management plans accordingly. This calls for a proactive strategy incorporating risk management into strategic planning and decision-making processes. Organizations can avoid possible dangers and seize opportunities in a fast-changing environment by regularly assessing and upgrading their risk management frameworks.

Technology is becoming more and more crucial to risk management and assessment. Organizations are changing how they identify and manage risks through advanced analytics, AI, and machine learning. With these technologies, businesses can analyze enormous volumes of data in real-time, spot trends and abnormalities, and more accurately forecast possible threats. For instance, predictive analytics can foresee market patterns and assist firms in getting ready for potential disruptions, while machine learning algorithms can identify anomalous transactions that can signal fraud. By utilizing these technologies, organizations can improve their risk management skills and make better judgments.

Reporting and communication are two more essential components of risk management. Establishing clear procedures for reporting risks and ensuring that pertinent information reaches the right stakeholders on time is vital for organizations. This covers external reporting to investors, regulators, and other stakeholders and internal reporting to senior management and the board. Open communication about risks and the steps taken to mitigate them shows stakeholders that a business is committed to efficient risk management and fosters confidence among them.

Effective risk management also requires cooperation and coordination between many organizational divisions and activities. Risks frequently affect several departments within the company, and their management necessitates the participation and collaboration of many departments, including finance, operations, IT, and legal. Coordinated efforts guarantee that risks are fully handled and that risk management initiatives align with the organization's goals. Risk committees and cross-functional teams that bring together people from several departments to discuss and manage risks can enable this engagement.

Organizations also need to be ready for crisis management and backup plans. Even with the greatest risk management practices, certain things that greatly affect the company can still happen. A strong crisis management plan guarantees the company can react efficiently to unforeseen circumstances. Clearly defined roles and duties, communication guidelines, and processes for maintaining vital operations should all be included in this plan. Regular exercises and simulations can assist in evaluating and improving the crisis management plan to ensure the company is ready for emergencies.

Risk assessment and management are essential procedures that help businesses overcome ambiguity and accomplish their goals. Organizations may minimize possible risks and take advantage of opportunities by recognizing, evaluating, and prioritizing risks, creating and implementing efficient risk management techniques, and cultivating a strong risk culture. Sustained surveillance, technological innovations, unambiguous communication, and cooperation amongst several departments augment the efficacy of risk mitigation endeavors. To stay competitive and resilient in a complex and dynamic world, companies must be alert and flexible, regularly updating their risk management frameworks as the risk landscape changes.

Developing Policies and Procedures

A key component of organizational management is the creation of policies and procedures, which act as the framework for efficient governance, operational coherence, and regulatory compliance. Policies give broad guidelines for organizational behavior and decision-making, while procedures specify how those guidelines should be implemented. Combined, they provide a disciplined framework that guarantees the accomplishment of organizational goals, the management of risks, and the preservation of standards. This section examines the value of setting policies and procedures and the essential elements and best practices for their creation and upkeep.

Because they clarify the organization's beliefs, objectives, and guiding principles, policies are crucial. They aid in coordinating individual actions with organizational goals by giving a broad overview of expectations in several contexts. An organization's ethical policy, for example, can specify standards for honesty, equity, and legal compliance, establishing a benchmark for worker behavior. Policies give decision-makers a clear point of reference for handling different scenarios, which helps to maintain consistency and fairness in the process. They also inform staff members, stakeholders, and outsiders about the organization's expectations and values.

Conversely, procedures convert policies into doable steps. They offer comprehensive guidance on carrying out particular operations or duties per the set policies. For instance, a company's procurement method would include submitting a buy request, getting approvals, and processing orders. In contrast, its procurement policy would stipulate that management must approve every purchase. Procedures guarantee that work is done accurately and consistently, which lowers the possibility of mistakes and increases overall operational performance.

A comprehensive requirements assessment is the first step in creating policies and procedures. This entails determining the domains in which policies and procedures are necessary, which may be motivated by several things, including organizational modifications, legislative requirements, or gaps in existing practices that have been found. An organization may need to create new rules and processes for international operations, such as compliance with local laws and cultural concerns if it is entering new markets. A needs assessment guarantees that policies and procedures address the unique needs and risks of the company and aid in prioritizing areas where they are most needed.

Drafting a policy or method comes next once its necessity has been determined. This entails drafting documents that successfully convey the goals and specifications of the policy or procedure clearly and succinctly. Effective policies should be drafted without legalese or complicated jargon so all employees can read and comprehend them. The policy's goals, duties, and extent should all be spelled out in detail. Step-by-step instructions, along with a breakdown of roles and responsibilities, deadlines, and any required paperwork or instruments, should be included in the procedures. Rules and procedures need to be organized such that they are simple to find and use in real-world situations.

An essential part of creating efficient rules and procedures is interacting with stakeholders. The involvement of pertinent parties guarantees that the policies and procedures are thorough, useful, and in line with organizational requirements. These parties include department leaders, staff members, and outside experts. Involving stakeholders increases buy-in and acceptability, which raises the possibility that the policies and procedures will be successfully implemented and followed. Stakeholder feedback can yield important insights into possible problems or opportunities for development, resulting in stronger and more efficient policies and procedures.

Policies and procedures should go through a rigorous review and approval process after they are drafted. Senior management or a designated policy committee will usually assess these to ensure they meet legal and regulatory standards and align with corporate objectives. The approval procedure aids in confirming the accuracy, comprehensiveness, and viability of the policies and procedures. It also offers a chance to remedy any reviewer issues or recommendations, guaranteeing that the finished documents are skillfully written and efficient.

Policies and procedures must be properly conveyed and implemented after they are approved. Disseminating the materials to all pertinent parties and ensuring they know their contents and ramifications constitute communication. Training sessions, corporate messaging, or specialized policy management systems can all help achieve this. They implement the rules and procedures into routine business activities, supply the required equipment or resources, and set up systems to ensure compliance. Implementing policies and procedures effectively guarantees that they are followed and that staff members know how to use them in their jobs.

Maintaining the applicability and efficacy of rules and processes requires regular monitoring and revision. Policies and procedures should be reviewed and updated regularly by organizations to take into account modifications to the operating procedures, organizational structure, or regulatory landscape. This entails monitoring modifications to laws and regulations, evaluating the effects of managerial changes, and obtaining user input. To ensure that policies and procedures are up to date and efficient in handling new risks and difficulties, periodic evaluations assist in identifying areas where they need to be modified or enhanced.

Another essential element of effective policy and process management is awareness and training. To ensure they understand their roles and how to comply, employees must get training on new or revised policies and procedures. Training curricula must be customized for various organizational levels and responsibilities, including pertinent data and useful advice. Constant awareness-raising and training campaigns support a culture of accountability and compliance by highlighting the significance of policies and procedures.

To sum up, creating policies and procedures is essential to organizational management since it offers the structure needed for efficient governance, unified operations, and regulatory compliance. Procedures provide specific instructions for implementing policies, whereas policies establish the fundamentals that direct behavior and decision-making. Evaluating needs, creating documentation, including stakeholders, and going through approval and review are all steps in the development process. Integrating policies and procedures into organizational practices necessitates effective communication, implementation, monitoring, and training. Organizations can improve their operational efficiency, reduce risks, and guarantee alignment with their strategic goals by allocating resources to develop and manage strong policies and procedures.

Role of Technology in Compliance

Technology has emerged as a critical instrument in assuring compliance across numerous industries in an era where regulatory landscapes are becoming more dynamic and complicated. Automation, data management, risk assessment, and reporting are just a few of technology's many functions in compliance. Technology is vital in helping firms manage compliance duties, improve transparency, and mitigate risks as they battle strict regulatory requirements and the demand for operational efficiency.

Automation is a major way that technology helps with compliance. In the past, compliance responsibilities included data input, document management, and compliance checks—labor-intensive procedures requiring a large amount of physical work. These days, automated technologies simplify these processes, relieving workers of some of their workload and significantly reducing the possibility of human error. For example, regular processes like tracking regulatory changes, updating policy papers, and producing compliance reports can be automated using compliance management systems. Organizations can ensure that they stay current with regulatory requirements and maintain correct records without requiring a lot of manual effort by automating these operations. Automation not only increases productivity but also makes compliance operations more accurate and consistent, providing a sense of relief from the burden of manual work.

Data management and analytics are another crucial component of technology's role in compliance. Managing enormous volumes of data, from transaction records to personnel information, is a common difficulty in modern compliance. Technology offers instruments for gathering, preserving, and evaluating this information in a manner that facilitates adherence to regulations. Integrating data management systems with compliance systems, such as customer relationship management (CRM) and enterprise resource planning (ERP) platforms, provides a complete picture of an organization's activities. With the help of this integration, enterprises can keep an eye on compliance across a range of functions, spot possible hazards, and ensure data handling procedures follow legal requirements. Furthermore, complex data sets may be interpreted, patterns can be found, and decisions can be made using data-driven insights thanks to advanced analytics solutions for enterprises. Ensuring compliance with data protection rules and proactive risk management requires this competence.

In assessing and managing risks, technology is also very important. Risks affecting an organization's capacity to comply with regulations are identified and evaluated as part of the compliance risk assessment process.

Technology helps with this process by offering advanced instruments for identifying, analyzing, and mitigating risks. Risk management software uses algorithms and data analytics to evaluate the possibility and impact of various compliance risks, such as operational failures or regulatory violations. These tools support firms in setting risk priorities, allocating resources wisely, and implementing risk mitigation plans. For instance, risk management systems are used by healthcare companies to guarantee that patient privacy laws are followed. At the same time, banking institutions utilize technology to monitor transactions for indications of fraud or money laundering. Organizations can take proactive steps to resolve possible compliance issues and better understand their risk picture by utilizing technology.

Technology greatly improves compliance reporting, documentation, automation, and risk management. Compliance reporting is the process of recording and informing stakeholders and regulatory authorities about an organization's compliance with legal standards. This frequently calls for thorough and accurate reporting. Technology streamlines this procedure by offering tools for creating, organizing, and retaining compliance reports. Reporting software can guarantee that submissions adhere to regulatory standards, automatically aggregate data from several sources, and provide reports in the necessary formats. This saves time and effort in the process of producing reports while also increasing their accuracy. Additionally, technology makes it easier to store and retrieve compliance documents securely, making data easily accessible for audits and inspections.

The integration of technology and regulatory compliance also facilitates continuous monitoring and improvement. Compliance is not a static process to adjust to shifting laws and new threats but calls for constant monitoring. Through real-time data analysis and warnings, technology allows for continuous monitoring of compliance operations. Compliance management systems can monitor modifications to regulations and alert firms to new needs, enabling them to make necessary updates to their policies and procedures. Along with identifying areas for improvement, continuous monitoring also entails evaluating the success of compliance measures. Technology offers resources for internal audits, stakeholder feedback, and compliance performance evaluation. Organizations may sustain successful compliance programs and adjust to changing regulatory environments with the support of this continual evaluation.

Technology also improves compliance information's usability and accessibility. Organizations must ensure that personnel at all levels have easy access to and comprehension of compliance information due to the growing complexity of legislation. Platforms like mobile applications and intranet portals made possible by technology make accessing policy documents, training materials, and compliance tools simple. By providing pertinent information according to user roles and responsibilities, these platforms may be tailored to ensure that staff members have the resources and understanding necessary to adhere to rules. Employees can access and comprehend pertinent content more easily when interactive features like search capabilities and FAQs are included in compliance information.

Technology's function in promoting cooperation and communication is another crucial component of compliance. Various departments, teams, and external stakeholders must frequently coordinate to ensure compliance. Through collaborative platforms for document sharing and project management, in addition to communication tools like email, instant messaging, and video conferencing, technology facilitates this kind of cooperation. Teams can collaborate efficiently, exchange data, and promptly handle compliance-related concerns with the help of these tools. Project management software, for instance, can be used by compliance teams to coordinate policy creation, handle tasks, and monitor the status of compliance projects. This emphasis on collaboration makes everyone feel connected and part of a team, enhancing the overall compliance process.

In summary, technology significantly contributes to increased compliance throughout enterprises through process automation, data management, risk assessment, and reporting facilitation. Automation from technology lowers the amount of manual labor needed for compliance duties while improving accuracy. Organizations may detect and resolve potential compliance concerns using risk management software, while data management and analytics offer useful insights for risk assessment and decision-making. Technology also streamlines compliance reporting, documentation, and continuous monitoring, ensuring organizations remain aligned with regulatory requirements. By improving accessibility, usability, and collaboration, technology supports effective compliance management and adaptation to changing regulatory environments. As regulations evolve and organizations face new challenges, leveraging technology will be essential for maintaining robust compliance programs and achieving operational excellence.

Continuous Improvement in Compliance Programs

Organizations must continuously develop compliance procedures to manage risks, comply with regulations, and uphold operational excellence in the ever-changing regulatory landscape. Continuous improvement entails the periodic assessment and enhancement of compliance programs to guarantee their continued efficacy, pertinence, and adaptability to evolving rules and organizational requirements. This strategy depends on maintaining a culture of responsibility and integrity within the company, staying ahead of developing risks, and adjusting to changing regulatory requirements.

An extensive evaluation of present processes is the first step towards continuous improvement in compliance initiatives. This evaluation aims to determine how well the current policies, practices, and controls handle regulatory obligations and mitigate compliance risks. Organizations frequently carry out internal audits, risk assessments, and performance reviews to determine their strengths, shortcomings, and areas for progress. These evaluations show any holes or weaknesses that need to be fixed and offer insightful information about how well the compliance program is operating. Organizations may ensure their processes align with industry best practices and regulatory standards by routinely evaluating their compliance programs.

Feedback mechanisms are one of the main pillars of continuous development. Comments from various stakeholders—such as staff members, clients, authorities, and auditors—offer insightful viewpoints on the success of compliance initiatives and point up areas needing improvement. Organizations can use surveys, interviews, focus groups, and other techniques to get input on how compliance rules and procedures are understood and implemented. By understanding the real-world difficulties and obstacles that stakeholders and workers encounter, organizations are better equipped to modify their compliance initiatives. The compliance program is kept current and efficient in tackling real-world problems by incorporating feedback into the improvement process.

A crucial facet of ongoing enhancement is the application of data analytics and performance indicators. Organizations can assess their compliance initiatives' efficacy and pinpoint improvement areas by creating key performance indicators (KPIs) and collecting pertinent metrics. Examples of performance metrics include the quantity of compliance issues, audit results, training completion rates, and the efficiency of controls. Data analytics tools can analyze these KPIs to reveal compliance performance, spot possible hazards, and assess the results of improvement projects. Organizations can make evidence-based decisions to improve compliance processes and tackle new challenges using data-driven insights.

Continuous progress is greatly aided by training and development. Employees must have the knowledge and abilities to follow new compliance requirements and successfully manage compliance risks when rules and organizational needs change. Providing ongoing training programs that cover new developments in compliance management and regulation changes is important. Workshops, seminars, e-learning courses, and other instructional materials are examples of training programs that give staff members the skills they need to comprehend and implement compliance rules and procedures. Organizations may maintain their workforce's knowledge, engagement, and competence to sustain compliance standards by investing in ongoing training and development.

Technology integration also helps compliance programs to improve continuously. Technology offers resources for organizing documents, automating compliance procedures, and monitoring compliance-related actions. Compliance management systems, for instance, can manage policy revisions, monitor regulatory changes, and produce reporting on compliance performance. Technology also makes it possible to monitor compliance activities in real time through dashboards and alerts, which enables firms to recognize and resolve potential problems quickly. By utilizing technology, organizations can successfully improve their capacity to manage compliance and adjust to shifting regulatory environments.

Support and dedication from the leadership are crucial for promoting ongoing compliance program improvement. Setting the example for compliance inside the company and displaying a commitment to moral conduct and legal observance are vital roles played by executives and senior management. To support leadership, it is important to set clear expectations, allocate the required resources, and promote an open and accountable culture. When managers prioritize compliance and actively participate in improvement projects, they foster a culture where staff members see the value of compliance and are inspired to contribute to continuing improvement projects.

Fostering an environment of transparency and accountability is another aspect of continuous development. A proactive compliance culture can be established by encouraging staff members to report compliance issues, provide suggestions, and participate in improvement projects. To safeguard whistleblowers, organizations should set up explicit routes for reporting problems and offer means of reporting anonymously. Organizations can improve their capacity to recognize and resolve compliance issues by fostering a culture where people are empowered to participate, and compliance is highly valued.

Maintaining the relevance and efficacy of compliance rules and processes requires regular evaluations and modifications. Policies and procedures must reflect new requirements and best practices as regulations and organizational operations change. It is important to set up regular review cycles to make sure compliance materials are up to date and compliant with regulations. This could entail adding lessons from previous events, updating procedures, and changing policies. By maintaining current compliance paperwork, firms may guarantee that their procedures remain efficient and adaptable to new hazards.

Continuous improvement is also supported by cooperation with regulatory agencies and outside specialists. Organizations can obtain insights into market trends and regulatory developments by interacting with regulatory bodies, industry groups, and legal consultants. Outside specialists can advise on optimal procedures, assist in deciphering complicated rules, and suggest improving compliance initiatives. Participating in industry forums and regulatory discussions enables firms to network with peers and stay current on developing challenges. Working with external stakeholders guarantees that an organization's compliance practices align with industry standards and helps it stay abreast of regulatory developments.

To sum up, firms must continuously enhance their compliance procedures to efficiently handle legal requirements, reduce risks, and preserve operational excellence. Organizations may improve the efficacy of their compliance programs by investing in technology and training, utilizing data analytics, developing feedback systems, and routinely evaluating present procedures. Additional supports include a culture of responsibility, leadership commitment, and frequent revisions to policies and procedures.

CHAPTER III

Navigating Industry-Specific Regulations

Healthcare Regulations

A vital framework for guaranteeing the effectiveness, safety, and quality of healthcare services is provided by healthcare regulations. These regulations govern the administration of healthcare institutions, the provision of treatment, the behavior of medical personnel, and the defense of patient rights. Regulations must change to meet new issues as healthcare systems develop and grow more complicated, including changing healthcare delivery methods, disease trends, and technology breakthroughs.

The certification and accreditation of healthcare facilities is one of the core facets of healthcare regulation. Hospitals and clinics, among other healthcare facilities, must achieve and uphold accreditation in numerous nations by adhering to regulatory organizations' specified requirements. These guidelines guarantee that healthcare institutions offer care that satisfies minimal standards for safety and quality. Facilities are evaluated by accrediting agencies, like The Joint Commission in the US, which conducts thorough inspections and assessments. Maintaining accreditation and guaranteeing patients receive high-quality care depends on adherence to these requirements. An essential part of hospital operations, accreditation also frequently affects government and insurance company payment rates.

Maintaining good standards of care also requires regulations about healthcare personnel. Healthcare professionals, such as doctors, nurses, and allied health workers, must meet licensing and certification standards to guarantee they have the knowledge, skills, and training to perform safely. These prerequisites differ according to the industry and the legal system, but they usually include passing qualifying tests, finishing CEUs, and upholding moral principles. For example, state medical and nursing boards are regulatory authorities overseeing the licensure process and dealing with professional behavior and competency matters. By implementing these regulations, authorities safeguard patients from inadequate care and ensure medical personnel fulfill their obligations.

Another important component of healthcare rules is the rights and protections of the patient. National and local regulations protect patients' rights to courteous, private, and egalitarian care. For instance, stringent rules for protecting patient health information are established under the Health Insurance Portability and Accountability Act (HIPAA) in the United States. Patients have the right to view their medical records and make correction requests, and HIPAA guarantees the confidentiality and security of personal health information. Informed consent is another area covered by regulations, which ensures patients have the freedom to choose their course of treatment and are fully informed about it. Regulations uphold moral principles in healthcare provision and encourage patient rights protection.

Controlling drugs and medical devices is an essential part of managing healthcare. Regulatory bodies, like the US Food and Drug Administration (FDA), assess the efficacy and safety of medications and medical devices before public release. Strict clinical studies, thorough scientific data analysis, and post-market monitoring are all part of this procedure to ensure the products are safe and function as intended. Regulations control these goods' production, labeling, and marketing to avoid disinformation and guarantee proper usage. Authorities ensure that discoveries benefit healthcare and help prevent harm to people by regulating drugs and medical equipment.

Efficiency-boosting and cost-controlling healthcare rules are also very important. Governments enact laws in several nations to control healthcare costs and guarantee that resources are allocated efficiently. Regulations could establish standards for healthcare delivery models, bargain for drug costs, and maintain reimbursement rates for medical services. These laws address concerns, including overusing services and needless procedures, to balance cost containment and quality care. Regulations contribute to the sustainability and accessibility of healthcare systems by encouraging cost-effectiveness and efficiency.

Potential and regulatory challenges are associated with integrating technology in healthcare. There are several advantages to telemedicine, electronic health records (EHRs), and other technology developments, including better data management and easier access to care. On the other hand, cautious regulation of these advances is also necessary to address privacy, security, and interoperability concerns. For example, telemedicine regulations must guarantee that remote care meets the same safety and quality requirements as in-person sessions. Rules about EHRs also cover patient consent, data security, and electronic record accuracy. It is imperative to balance technology's advantages and regulatory obligations to maximize the benefits of technological breakthroughs while minimizing potential risks.

In the healthcare industry, meeting the requirements of vulnerable groups—such as people with long-term care needs, disabilities, and chronic illnesses—is another aspect of regulatory compliance. Regulations frequently contain clauses that redress inequities, guarantee fair access to care, and offer support services. Regulations could, for instance, set requirements for healthcare facilities' accessibility, mandate that caregivers have certain training, and guarantee that services are accessible to marginalized people. Regulations contribute to developing a more fair and inclusive healthcare system that satisfies the various requirements of every person by concentrating on these factors.

International regulatory considerations sometimes confront healthcare systems in addition to domestic restrictions. Global regulatory standards must be coordinated and aligned due to globalization and the cross-border nature of healthcare. International organizations that work to unify legislation linked to health emergencies, disease control, and the global sharing of health information include the World Health Organization (WHO) and numerous regional health authorities. Cooperation and information exchange across nations aid in addressing issues related to global health and guarantee uniform and efficient regulatory procedures.

In summary, healthcare rules guarantee healthcare systems' security, excellence, and effectiveness. They include a broad spectrum of topics, such as cost control, patient safety, professional licensure, facility accreditation, and pharmaceutical oversight. Regulations must change as healthcare develops to meet new opportunities and problems, such as global healthcare trends and technological breakthroughs.

Financial Services Regulations

To maintain stability, honesty, and justice in the financial markets, financial services laws are an essential component of the global financial system. Financial institutions, such as banks, insurance companies, investment firms, and other businesses that offer financial services and products, are subject to these restrictions. The major goals of laws governing financial services are to safeguard investors, uphold investor trust, and advance economic stability. Regulatory frameworks must change as financial markets develop and become more complex to handle new risks and difficulties.

Preserving financial stability is the major objective of laws governing financial services. Financial institutions are essential to the economy because they handle investments, extend loans, and facilitate transactions. However, because financial markets are interrelated, problems in one organization or industry can easily spread and affect the larger financial system. Regulatory frameworks create requirements for risk management, liquidity, and capital sufficiency to reduce systemic risk. For instance, banks must maintain adequate capital buffers and liquidity to withstand financial stress and economic downturns, according to the Basel III framework. The purpose of these restrictions is to lessen the possibility of bank collapses and the risk of the financial system spreading.

Another important component of financial services legislation is consumer protection. Consumers may face considerable financial risk when using complicated financial goods and services. Regulations are in place to guarantee that financial institutions treat customers fairly and honestly. For instance, the United States Consumer Financial Protection Bureau (CFPB) was founded by the Dodd-Frank Wall Street Reform and Consumer Protection Act and is responsible for monitoring mortgage, credit card, and other financial product practices. The CFPB's role encompasses enforcing regulations to safeguard consumers against unscrupulous tactics, guaranteeing that they obtain precise and unambiguous information regarding financial products, and offering recourse procedures to settle complaints. Consumer protection laws contribute to developing confidence in the financial markets and guard against exploitation by fostering fairness and openness.

Another essential goal of financial services laws is market integrity. To maintain market integrity, regulations must ensure that financial markets run effectively, transparently, and fairly for all players. This entails establishing guidelines for acceptable behavior in the market, stopping fraud, and upholding norms for financial disclosure and reporting. For example, the United States Securities and Exchange Commission (SEC) was founded by the Securities Exchange Act of 1934 to monitor the securities markets and enforce laws about financial reporting, insider trading, and market manipulation. These rules contribute to the preservation of investor trust and the efficient operation of markets by preserving market integrity.

Financial institutions are subject to regulation, which includes monitoring their governance, risk management, and adherence to legal requirements. Financial institutions must comply with several legal criteria, including keeping sufficient capital reserves, establishing strong risk management systems, and following anti-money laundering (AML) and counterterrorism financing (CTF) protocols. These standards are overseen by regulatory entities, which include international organizations like the Financial Stability Board (FSB) and national financial regulatory agencies. Regular inspections and audits are carried out to guarantee compliance. Sustaining the general stability of the economic system, safeguarding stakeholder interests, and preventing wrongdoing are all made possible by effective regulation of financial institutions.

International collaboration is important for the regulation of financial services in addition to national laws. The financial markets are increasingly globalized, with cross-border transactions and global financial institutions operating in several jurisdictions. Because of this globalization, regulators must work together to manage hazards that cross national borders. International regulatory organizations that work to foster uniformity and harmonization between nations include the International Organization of Securities Commissions (IOSCO) and the Basel Committee on Banking Supervision. International frameworks play a crucial role in mitigating global financial risks, including those emanating from multinational banks and global financial crises, while promoting collaboration among regulators across borders.

Regulations about financial services must also change to reflect innovations and technological breakthroughs in the industry. The emergence of blockchain technology, digital currencies, and fintech brings new possibilities and difficulties for financial regulation. Regulators must create frameworks that address the special risks of these technologies and provide an atmosphere that encourages technical progress. For instance, laws governing cryptocurrencies and initial coin offerings (ICOs) are changing to address problems including fraud, regulatory arbitrage, and volatile markets. Similar considerations for cybersecurity, data privacy, and consumer protection apply to the regulation of online financial services and digital banking. Regulators must balance the desire for innovation and the necessity to safeguard consumers and maintain market stability as technology continues transforming the financial sector.

Regulatory compliance is a major worry for financial institutions, which must manage a complicated web of rules and regulations. Implementing procedures and safeguards to abide by legal requirements and control regulatory risk is known as compliance. Financial institutions frequently engage in compliance programs to ensure they fulfill their regulatory responsibilities, including employee training, internal audits, and monitoring systems. Significant fines, harm to one's reputation, and interruptions to operations are all possible outcomes of non-compliance. Thus, maintaining efficient compliance frameworks is crucial to controlling regulatory risk and preserving financial institutions' long-term existence.

Resolving and recovering financially troubled firms is crucial to financial services regulation. Regulations offer a way to protect the larger economic system and resolve insolvencies in the case of an economic crisis or institutional failure. Principles for the orderly resolution of failed institutions are outlined in the Financial Stability Board's Key Attributes of Effective Resolution Regimes for Financial Institutions. These include maintaining financial stability, limiting public bailouts, and ensuring vital operations continue. These resolution mechanisms aid in the orderly reorganization or liquidation of troubled organizations and help control the effects of failures on the financial system.

To sum up, rules governing financial services are essential to maintaining the financial system's integrity, stability, and equity. Regulatory frameworks contribute to a strong and reliable financial system by enacting laws that protect consumers, uphold market integrity, and ensure financial stability. Regulations must change to handle international collaboration, technological improvements, compliance concerns, and the emergence of new difficulties in the financial markets. Financial services rules help create a strong and stable financial system that underpins economic growth and stability by balancing the necessity for innovation and protecting stakeholders' interests.

Environmental Regulations

Modern environmental policy is based on ecological rules intended to preserve natural resources, defend public health, and lessen the negative effects of human activity on the environment. These rules cover a broad spectrum of guidelines and standards intended to control pollution, preserve ecosystems, and encourage environmentally friendly behavior. Global environmental issues are becoming more complicated, and regulatory frameworks must change to meet new challenges and guarantee a balanced approach to environmental stewardship.

Controlling and reducing pollution is the main goal of environmental regulations because it can hurt air, water, and soil quality. Pollutant emissions from automobiles, industrial facilities, and other sources are restricted by laws controlling air quality, such as the Clean Air Act in the US. These laws are intended to stop dangerous pollutants from deteriorating air quality, causing respiratory issues, environmental harm, and climate change. Examples of these pollutants include sulfur dioxide, nitrogen oxides, and particle matter. Environmental rules work to preserve human health and improve air quality by enforcing strict emission standards and encouraging the use of greener technology.

Regulations governing water quality are crucial for maintaining the safety of drinking water and the well-being of aquatic ecosystems. For example, the Clean Water Act establishes water quality standards and controls the release of pollutants into surface waters. According to this law, businesses and local governments must apply for permits before releasing pollutants into the air and take steps to lessen contamination. Hazardous material handling, wastewater treatment, and the preservation of riparian zones and wetlands are further topics covered by regulations. Environmental rules assist in preventing waterborne diseases, safeguard aquatic life, and preserve vital water resources by upholding strict standards for water quality.

Preventing land deterioration and encouraging sustainable land management techniques are the main goals of land use regulations and soil conservation. Land contamination, deforestation, and erosion are some of the problems these policies deal with. For instance, the Superfund Act, commonly known as the Comprehensive Environmental Response, Compensation, and Liability Act (CERCLA), offers a framework for handling hazardous waste and cleaning polluted areas. Zoning and land use planning regulations contribute to controlling development and reducing negative environmental effects. Environmental rules contribute to preserving soil health and preventing ecological deterioration by encouraging actions like reforestation, sustainable agriculture, and responsible land development.

The creation and implementation of environmental standards and permits constitute a fundamental aspect of environmental regulation. Environmental standards provide precise thresholds for pollutants and toxins, offering unambiguous guidelines for adherence. Contrarily, permitting systems mandate that organizations and other entities get permission before any operations that might hurt the environment.

Conditions and procedures for tracking, disclosing, and managing emissions or discharges are frequently included in these licenses. The responsibilities of regulatory agencies, such as the European Environment Agency (EEA) or the Environmental Protection Agency (EPA) in the United States, are setting standards, granting licenses, and guaranteeing adherence to environmental regulations.

Fundamental tenets of environmental regulation include transparency and public participation. Public comment periods, hearings, and consultations are just a few ways the public can participate in decision-making procedures included in many regulatory regimes. These systems ensure that different viewpoints are considered by enabling people and communities to offer feedback on proposed laws, initiatives, and policies. Involvement from the public promotes more responsibility, addresses community problems, and strengthens the legitimacy of regulatory decisions. Transparent regulatory systems benefit from public access to information regarding environmental risks, compliance, and enforcement.

A further crucial component of environmental control is environmental impact assessments or EIAs. Before new projects or developments are allowed, they are carefully examined for potential ecological implications using Environmental Impact Assessments, or EIAs. EIAs assist in identifying strategies to mitigate adverse effects and guarantee that projects are planned to minimize environmental harm by evaluating the possible consequences on air, water, soil, and ecosystems. This proactive approach to environmental management encourages sustainable growth methods and aids in damage prevention. Large-scale industrial operations, infrastructure projects, and other important projects that could influence the environment frequently need to complete environmental impact assessments or EIAs.

Enforcing compliance and accomplishing regulatory goals depend on the enforcement of environmental regulations. Regulatory bodies use a range of instruments and tactics, such as monitoring programs, fines for infractions, and inspections, to keep an eye on and enforce compliance. Monitoring compliance is monitoring emissions, discharges, and other environmental indicators to ensure regulated businesses follow the terms of their permits and requirements. When infractions are found, agencies can enforce the law by imposing penalties, mandating remedies, or initiating court cases. Enforcing regulations effectively aids in addressing environmental damage, discouraging noncompliance, and maintaining the integrity of regulatory frameworks.

The importance of international cooperation in tackling the world's environmental problems is growing. Numerous ecological issues, such as ocean pollution, biodiversity loss, and climate change, cut across national borders and necessitate international cooperation. International agreements that set worldwide aims for environmental conservation and create frameworks for cooperative action include the Convention on Biological Diversity and the Paris Agreement on Climate Change. These accords give nations a foundation to collaborate, exchange data, and implement strategies to deal with transboundary environmental concerns. International cooperation also entails harmonizing rules and standards to promote trade and guarantee uniform environmental standards throughout national borders.

One of the most important components of contemporary environmental regulation is the combination of economic and environmental factors. Several legislative systems recognize that sustainable practices can spur economic growth and innovation and seek to strike a balance between environmental protection and development. For instance, market-based strategies, like carbon pricing and cap-and-trade programs, provide financial incentives for cutting emissions and using greener technology. Regulators can encourage businesses to invest in environmentally friendly practices and support sustainable development by integrating environmental factors into economic decision-making.

Environmental regulation effectiveness, equality, and implementation are frequently the focus of challenges and critiques. Some critics contend that rules could cause economic inefficiencies and unfair business costs, especially small ones. Some express doubts regarding the effectiveness of agencies in enforcing regulations and the suitability of regulatory standards. To meet these problems, regulatory frameworks must be continuously evaluated and adjusted to ensure that their intended purposes are met while also considering the demands and concerns of diverse stakeholders.

In summary, environmental laws are essential for safeguarding the public's health, preserving natural resources, and advancing sustainable development. Regulations contribute to environmental protection and responsible behavior by establishing guidelines for land use, pollution management, and environmental impact assessments. The efficacy of ecological control is further enhanced by international cooperation, openness, and public participation. Regulatory frameworks must change to address new problems and strike a balance between environmental preservation and economic development as ecological challenges continue to change. We may strive toward a future for the environment and society that is more robust and sustainable through efficient regulation and cooperative efforts.

Data Protection and Privacy Regulations

Data protection and privacy regulations are essential elements of modern government, as they reflect society's growing dependence on digital technologies and the ensuing necessity to secure personal data. These laws set guidelines for how businesses gather, handle, store, and distribute information to safeguard people's privacy and personal data security. The legislative frameworks need to adapt to new issues and risks to data protection as the digital ecosystem does.

The fundamental tenet of data protection laws is safeguarding individuals' private information against exploitation and unapproved access. Any information that may be used to identify a specific person, such as names, addresses, social security numbers, and financial information, is considered personal data. Regulations ensure businesses handle this data ethically and transparently while upholding individuals' rights and privacy. One comprehensive data protection regulation example is the General Data Protection Regulation (GDPR), implemented in the European Union in 2018. It requires that before processing an individual's data, businesses must get that person's express consent, be transparent about its use, and ensure the data is kept safe.

Additionally, the GDPR gives people particular rights about personal data. These rights include the ability to access their data, request corrections of their data, and, in certain situations, request that their data be deleted. These laws provide people more authority over their data and enable them to hold businesses responsible for their data practices. The rule also imposes strict guidelines on data breach notifications, mandating that firms promptly notify affected parties and regulators of any breaches.

Other countries have also enacted privacy and data protection laws in addition to the GDPR. A disorganized system of federal and state laws governs data protection in the United States. One notable example is the California Consumer Privacy Act (CCPA), which grants citizens of California rights akin to those found in the GDPR, such as the capacity to access, erase, and withdraw their consent from having their data sold. Another important law is the Health Insurance Portability and Accountability Act (HIPAA), primarily concerned with safeguarding patient data and ensuring that healthcare organizations and providers manage it safely.

Organizations must frequently develop strong data management policies to comply with data protection rules. This entails conducting routine data protection impact assessments (DPIAs) to analyze any possible hazards related to data processing operations and implementing suitable countermeasures. Establishing rules and processes for handling data, training staff, and making sure outside contractors follow data protection laws are all mandated by organizations. These procedures assist firms in upholding regulatory compliance and protecting private information from theft and unauthorized use.

Finding a balance between the need for data gathering and analysis and privacy is one of the major issues facing data protection. Delivering services, increasing productivity, and spurring innovation depend on data-driven insights in various industries, including marketing, banking, and healthcare. On the other hand, concerns about people's security and privacy might arise from excessive or inappropriate data collecting. By imposing restrictions on data collecting and requiring enterprises to justify the need and purpose of their data processing operations, data protection regulations aim to address this problem. For instance, firms must adhere to the GDPR's data minimization principle, which states that they must only gather information essential for their particular needs and refrain from keeping more information than is necessary.

Another complicated data protection issue is international data transfers. Businesses frequently conduct business internationally and may need to move personal data across nations. International data transfers are restricted by laws like the GDPR to guarantee the protection of personal data wherever it is processed. Under the GDPR, data transfers to non-EU nations are permitted only if those nations have relevant data protection laws or if binding company policies or standard contractual provisions are in place. This guarantees that personal information is safe throughout overseas transfers.

Ensuring that organizations fulfill their commitments and preserving the integrity of regulatory frameworks depends on implementing data protection legislation. Regulatory agencies, like the Federal Trade Commission (FTC) in the US or the Information Commissioner's Office (ICO) in the UK, are responsible for monitoring compliance, looking into complaints, and pursuing legal action against businesses that break data protection regulations. Repercussions for non-compliance can be severe, including fines, penalties, and harm to one's reputation. Encouraging compliance, preventing infractions, and protecting people's rights to data protection are all made possible by effective enforcement.

Data protection and privacy face new issues due to developing trends and technological breakthroughs like big data analytics and artificial intelligence (AI). Large data sets are frequently used by AI technology for training and decision-making, which raises questions about data utilization, transparency, and potential biases. Similarly, big data analytics may entail gathering and examining enormous databases, some of which may contain personal data. Provisions addressing the privacy and ethical ramifications of emerging technologies must be added to data protection laws to meet these issues. To guarantee that privacy considerations are incorporated into the creation and implementation of new technologies, the GDPR, for instance, has obligations for data protection by design and default.

Strong data protection measures are essential, as seen by increased data breaches and cyberattacks. Hackers, ransomware attacks, and other cybersecurity hazards that jeopardize personal data are becoming more and more of a concern to organizations. To comply with data protection rules, organizations must frequently have robust security measures to safeguard data from unauthorized access and breaches, including encryption, access controls, and incident response plans. Organizations must follow certain protocols to disclose and mitigate the impact in case of a breach, including informing affected parties and authorities. Organizations may lower the risk of security breaches and protect people's personal information by making cybersecurity and data protection their top priorities.

To sum up, data protection and privacy laws are essential for guaranteeing the ethical management of personal data and safeguarding people's privacy in the digital era. These laws provide people rights over their data while establishing guidelines for data gathering, processing, and security through extensive frameworks like the CCPA and GDPR. Overcoming persistent obstacles that necessitate constant legislative adaptation include balancing privacy and data-driven innovation, handling multinational data transfers, and keeping up with technical advancements. Organizations may preserve trust, reduce risks, and support a safe and courteous digital environment by upholding data protection rules and prioritizing cybersecurity.

Emerging Industry Regulations

Governments and regulatory agencies are working to meet the special opportunities and problems that these industries bring. As a result, emerging industry rules are reshaping the landscape of new and developing sectors. Regulations must change when new industries and technological advancements occur to maintain compliance, safety, and equity while encouraging creativity. The development of rules in important growing industries, including technology, biotechnology, and green energy, is examined in this section, along with the effects these rules have on consumers and enterprises.

The technology industry is under intense regulatory scrutiny, especially with the emergence of blockchain, artificial intelligence (AI), and the Internet of Things (IoT). Despite AI's potential to transform many industries, questions about ethics, accountability, and transparency are also raised. To address concerns like algorithmic bias, data privacy, and responsibility for AI-driven judgments, regulations in this field are changing. For example, the Artificial Intelligence Act of the European Union suggests a legal framework to categorize AI systems according to their risk levels, necessitating greater inspection for high-risk applications like vital infrastructure and healthcare. This strategy will balance innovation with the need to control risks and safeguard the general welfare.

Cryptocurrencies and blockchain technologies also pose regulatory issues. Blockchain's decentralized structure can make regulatory monitoring more difficult, especially regarding data protection and financial transactions. While promoting the advantages of blockchain technology, governments are looking into regulatory measures to solve problems, including fraud, money laundering, and investor protection. Rules about cryptocurrency exchanges and initial coin offerings (ICOs) are being drafted to maintain transparency and safeguard investors. To promote international coherence in regulatory strategies, the Financial Action Task Force (FATF) has furnished guidance for nations to draft legislation that tackles the money laundering threats linked to cryptocurrencies.

The Internet of Things (IoT) sector, which uses the Internet to link different systems and devices, also has to deal with privacy and data security regulations. Regulations are required to guarantee that the copious volumes of sensitive and personal data collected and transmitted by IoT devices are shielded from breaches and unwanted access. IoT data processing is subject to the General Data Protection Regulation (GDPR) in the European Union, which mandates that businesses have robust data protection mechanisms in place and get individuals' agreement before collecting personal data. To further guarantee the security and dependability of IoT devices, industry-specific standards, and guidelines are developing to handle their interoperability and security.

Another industry that is being greatly impacted by new restrictions is biotechnology. Biotechnology advancements like synthetic biology and genetic editing raise difficult safety and ethical questions. The main goal of regulations in this area is to guarantee responsible development and application of biotechnological breakthroughs. For instance, evaluating the possible hazards to the environment and human health, as well as the ethical issues surrounding genetic alterations, is part of regulating genetic editing technologies like CRISPR. To balance innovation and the need to safeguard public health, the U.S. Food and Drug Administration (FDA) and other regulatory agencies are developing frameworks and recommendations for the moral and safely using of biotechnologies.

As governments and organizations work to combat climate change and promote environmental sustainability, new rules are also emerging in the green energy and sustainability sectors. This regulation field is concerned with lowering greenhouse gas emissions, supporting renewable energy sources, and fostering environmentally friendly behaviors. For instance, national and regional laws about energy production and use are influenced by the Paris Agreement, which establishes worldwide goals for cutting carbon emissions and limiting the rise in global temperatures. Regulations like the European Union's Green Deal also seek to establish sustainability and energy efficiency standards, encourage the shift to a low-carbon economy, and stimulate investment in green technologies.

One of the main areas of concentration for the green energy industry is the regulation of renewable energy technology and electric vehicles (EVs). Governments are putting laws into place to encourage the use of electric vehicles (EVs) by establishing limits for emissions, offering incentives, and funding the infrastructure needed for charging EVs. Comparably, rules about grid integration, energy storage, and environmental impact assessments are being formulated to facilitate the expansion of renewable energy sources like solar and wind power. These laws support ecological preservation, encourage the development of green technology, and lessen dependency on fossil fuels.

Emerging industry laws must also consider the international scope of these sectors. Since many developing industries are transnational, international coordination and collaboration in regulatory methods are necessary. Harmonizing legislation and fostering consistency across different locations are important goals of global agreements and standards, such as those established by the International Telecommunication Union (ITU) and the International Organization for Standardization (ISO). International cooperation promotes the development and global implementation of new technologies and addresses cross-border issues like data security and privacy.

With the emergence of new technology and developments, the regulatory environment for developing industries is constantly changing. To create regulations that effectively address new risks and possibilities, regulatory authorities must keep up with industry developments and technology advancements. Developing rules that balance innovation and safety, ethics, and the public interest requires interacting with industry stakeholders, carrying out impact assessments, and encouraging communication between regulators and innovators.

In summary, new industry laws are critical to meeting the special opportunities and problems of developing and new sectors. Regulations must change to maintain safety, justice, and compliance while promoting innovation as technology evolves and new sectors emerge, such as biotechnology, blockchain, artificial intelligence, and green energy. Governments and regulatory agencies can safeguard public interests, encourage the responsible development of emerging businesses, and contribute to a sustainable and just future by creating and enforcing efficient regulatory frameworks.

CHAPTER IV

Implementing Compliance Strategies

Training and Education for Compliance

Effective compliance programs must include teaching and training to guarantee that management, stakeholders, and staff know and abide by organizational and regulatory standards. Organizations must engage in extensive training and instructional programs as sectors change and rules become more complex to reduce risks, encourage compliance, and prevent infractions. This section examines successful programs' components, ongoing improvement tactics, and the significance of compliance education and training.

The main objective of compliance education and training is to give people the information and abilities they need to abide by laws, rules, and internal policies. Employees who receive quality training can better comprehend their roles, identify compliance issues, and implement best practices into their everyday work. Organizations may avoid misconceptions, lessen the chance of infractions, and promote an ethical culture by making compliance standards plain and easily available.

Several essential components are usually present in a well-designed compliance training program. First and foremost, the training material must be pertinent and specially designed to meet the company's and its staff's unique requirements. This entails determining which internal regulations and legal requirements apply most to the various positions and responsibilities inside the company. A financial services company would concentrate its training on fraud prevention and anti-money laundering (AML) rules, whereas a healthcare institution might prioritize patient privacy and data protection.

Second, training should be given via various delivery techniques to maximize engagement and suit multiple learning styles. Webinars, interactive modules, and online courses can augment traditional classroom-based training. Online learning environments provide employees with flexibility and remote access, allowing them to complete training at their own pace. Interactive components that let users apply their knowledge to actual situations, including case studies and quizzes, can improve comprehension and recall.

Thirdly, regular tests to gauge staff members' comprehension of compliance principles and practical application should be a part of well-designed training programs. Tests, quizzes, and practical exercises are examples of assessments that can be used to gauge understanding and pinpoint areas needing development. The evaluation results can be utilized to improve the training material and fill up any knowledge gaps.

Furthermore, training must be a continuous procedure instead of a one-time occurrence. Organizations must ensure their training programs are regularly updated to consider the continuously changing regulations and rules. Employees who receive ongoing education are better able to stay current on best practices, new laws, and emerging threats. Organizations should also offer refresher courses and frequent updates to address any new developments in the regulatory landscape and reinforce important compliance ideas.

Effective leadership and an unwavering commitment to compliance from the top down are essential for compliance training to be successful. Setting an example for compliance and stressing the value of following rules and policies are important tasks for senior management. Leaders should express the organization's commitment to compliance, demonstrate ethical behavior, and actively support and engage in training activities. This top-down strategy aids in fostering a culture that values and prioritizes compliance.

Organizations should offer employees continuous assistance and resources to help them handle compliance concerns, in addition to formal training programs. This can involve having access to rules, compliance manuals, and a team or officer assigned to compliance. A compliance officer can offer advice on complicated matters and be a point of contact for staff members with queries or concerns. Employees can also be updated on news and changes relating to compliance and regulations by regular communication, such as newsletters or updates.

To make sure that training and education initiatives provide the desired results, it is critical to assess their efficacy. Organizations should evaluate and review them regularly to determine if their training initiatives are fulfilling their objectives and attending to the needs of their workforce. This may entail reviewing assessment data, obtaining participant comments, and monitoring compliance metrics. Based on these evaluations, training programs can be continuously improved, which helps to maintain their efficacy over time and improves their relevance and quality.

Meeting the varied demands of a global workforce is one of the difficulties in providing training and education for compliance. Businesses with international operations have to deal with diverse regulatory frameworks and cultural disparities. Training programs should be modified to consider regional laws and cultural norms while adhering to the organization's overarching compliance goals to overcome this difficulty. This may entail creating training modules tailored to a certain region, offering translation and localization services, and hiring professionals in local compliance to guarantee that training is applicable and efficient.

There are many advantages to incorporating technology into compliance training, such as enhanced flexibility, engagement, and accessibility. Mobile applications, virtual reality simulations, and e-learning platforms can improve employee access to training resources and the overall training experience. Additionally, technology may make data management and reporting easier, allowing employers to follow training progress, spot trends, and guarantee that training standards are being met.

Organizations must be aware of potential obstacles, such as guaranteeing data security and safeguarding training participants' privacy, even with all the benefits of technology. Strong cybersecurity measures and compliance with data protection laws are important to protect sensitive data and preserve the integrity of the training process.

To sum up, good compliance programs must include education and training since they assist businesses in managing risks, adhering to regulations, and fostering an ethical culture. A thorough training program should consist of many distribution modalities and ongoing updates and be interesting, relevant, and flexible. Strong leadership, continuous resources, and technology can help support training, increase its efficacy, and ensure staff members are prepared to handle compliance concerns. Organizations may prevent infractions, foster a compliance culture, and support long-term success by funding comprehensive training and education programs.

Monitoring and Auditing Compliance

An effective compliance program must include monitoring and auditing to ensure that firms follow internal policies and regulatory standards while spotting and resolving possible problems. These procedures support an organization's compliance culture, risk mitigation, and accountability. Sufficient surveillance and examination offer perceptions into adherence to regulations, facilitate prompt remedial measures and encourage ongoing enhancement.

Monitoring is the continuous process of keeping tabs on daily adherence to rules and guidelines. It entails the ongoing monitoring of activities, transactions, and operations to ensure they conform to legal requirements and accepted norms. Numerous techniques, such as automated systems, manual assessments, and routine reporting, can be used for monitoring.

Automated monitoring solutions are essential for preserving compliance since they offer real-time oversight and notify businesses of possible problems. Financial institutions, for instance, frequently utilize computerized systems to monitor transactions for indications of fraud or money laundering. These systems identify suspicious activity and provide alerts for additional inquiry by analyzing patterns and abnormalities in transaction data. Automated monitoring makes it easier for businesses to detect compliance problems and handle massive amounts of data quickly.

Manual monitoring entails human supervision and examination of procedures and undertakings. This can involve regular assessments, tests, and checks by internal auditors or compliance officers. Manual tracking is crucial for employee conduct, adherence to ethical standards, and compliance with internal policies—areas that automated systems would find difficult to monitor—the manual monitoring component of monitoring is regular reporting. Organizations should set up systems for gathering and examining information about compliance performance. This involves producing reports on important compliance data, like the number of policy infractions, the progress of corrective measures, and the outcomes of compliance audits. Organizations may spot trends, monitor compliance progress, and make well-informed decisions with the support of regular reporting.

On the other hand, auditing is a more formal, recurring procedure that thoroughly assesses an organization's adherence to rules and guidelines. To evaluate the efficacy of the compliance program, audits are usually carried out by internal or external auditors and entail a thorough examination of documents, procedures, and controls.

An organization's audit team conducts internal audits to assess how well internal controls and compliance protocols work. Internal auditors evaluate if the company adheres to external regulations and its rules and processes. They might conduct audits on particular topics, such as data security, operational procedures, or financial operations, and offer suggestions for enhancements.

Independent third-party auditors conduct external audits to evaluate an organization's adherence to external legislation and industry norms. External audits ensure the company adheres to regulatory requirements by offering an unbiased assessment of compliance activities. For instance, an external audit may be conducted by a business governed by the Sarbanes-Oxley Act (SOX) to confirm the accuracy of its financial statements and the efficiency of its internal controls.

There are various important steps in both internal and external audits. Planning is usually the first step in the audit process, during which auditors specify the audit's goals, objectives, and methodology. Fieldwork is the next step, during which auditors gather and evaluate data, examine documents, and conduct interviews. Auditors write a report outlining their findings, conclusions, and recommendations after finishing the fieldwork. Following the audit report's presentation, top management and the board of directors are responsible for resolving flaws and taking corrective measures.

A clear compliance framework outlining the organization's policies, processes, and responsibilities is necessary for efficient monitoring and auditing. This framework should have precise instructions for monitoring and auditing operations and standards for assessing compliance performance. In addition, it ought to specify the obligations of auditors, compliance officers, and other process participants.

Ensuring these tasks are carried out thoroughly and consistently is one of the difficulties in monitoring and auditing compliance. Organizations must set up systematic, routine monitoring and auditing systems to prevent gaps or overlooks. Organizations should also train and develop their audit and compliance staff to ensure they have the abilities and know-how to carry out their responsibilities successfully.

Managing the possible effects of audits and monitoring on organizational activities presents another difficulty. Resource-intensive monitoring and auditing efforts may disrupt regular business operations. Organizations need to strike a balance between the necessity of maintaining operational efficiency and comprehensive compliance management. This can be accomplished by ensuring compliance efforts align with corporate objectives, utilizing technology to expedite procedures, and incorporating monitoring and auditing activities into regular operations.

Ongoing enhancement is an essential component of both audits and monitoring. Businesses should enhance their compliance programs using the knowledge gathered from monitoring and auditing operations. This entails evaluating audit results, determining the underlying reasons for compliance problems, and putting remedial measures in place to close found gaps. Updating policies and procedures in light of audit and monitoring activity lessons is another aspect of continuous improvement.

Organizations can improve training initiatives, fortify internal controls, and fine-tune compliance plans using input from monitoring and auditing operations. Organizations may manage emerging risks, adjust to changing regulatory requirements, and uphold a strong compliance posture by cultivating a culture of continuous improvement.

To sum up, monitoring and auditing are crucial elements of a successful compliance program since they offer continuous supervision and recurrent assessments of an organization's compliance with rules and guidelines. Organizations can detect and resolve compliance concerns, guarantee accountability, and promote continuous development using automated systems, manual reviews, regular reporting, and formal audits. Organizations can reduce risks, prevent regulatory infractions, and foster a compliance and ethical culture by investing in strong monitoring and auditing procedures.

Handling Compliance Violations

Managing compliance infractions is essential to maintaining a successful compliance program and guaranteeing that a company abides by internal, legal, and regulatory requirements. Organizations that experience violations must act quickly to resolve the problem, minimize any harm, and stop it from happening again. The process of handling compliance infractions is examined in this section, along with the procedures involved, effective resolution techniques, and the significance of taking a proactive approach to controlling compliance risks.

Finding and reporting compliance problems as soon as possible is the first step in handling them. The first step in this procedure is to set up systems for looking for possible infractions. Companies should implement monitoring mechanisms, conduct routine audits, and encourage staff members to raise issues through private channels. Efficient avenues of communication, including internal reporting systems or whistleblower hotlines, enable staff members to report infractions without worrying about facing reprisals. Maintaining a strong compliance culture requires ensuring staff members are informed about these reporting channels and recognize the significance of reporting such infractions.

A violation must be reported to the relevant organization authorities as soon as it is discovered. Usually, this entails informing senior management, the legal department, or the compliance officer. Early reporting enables the company to look into the matter and deal with the problem before it worsens. Inaction on the part of the organization may lead to higher risks, fines from the authorities, and reputational harm.

Conducting a comprehensive investigation is the next step that follows reporting a violation. Conducting an inquiry entails obtaining and evaluating evidence, speaking with pertinent parties, and determining the severity of the infraction. Finding the facts should be the main goal of an impartial investigation. To guarantee a thorough and unbiased evaluation, enlisting skilled professionals like external investigators, legal experts, or internal auditors is imperative.

The organization should assess the seriousness of the infraction, its effect on the organization, and any possible legal or regulatory ramifications during the investigation. The right course of action and necessary level of response are identified with the aid of this assessment. A more major infraction might call for legal action or regulatory notifications, whereas a minor infraction might be resolved with corrective measures and extra training.

Following the conclusion of the investigation, the organization needs to address the violation and stop it from happening again. Revisions to internal controls, policy and procedure revisions, and staff training can all be considered corrective measures. The objective is to strengthen the organization's compliance framework and address the concerns that have been discovered.

The organization should concentrate on remediation activities and remedial actions to remedy any harm caused by the violation. This could entail paying out compensation to impacted parties, putting policies in place to stop similar incidents from happening again, and being open and honest with stakeholders. For instance, in a data breach, the company might have to notify the impacted parties, provide credit monitoring services, and strengthen data security protocols.

Taking disciplinary action against those responsible for compliance violations is a common step in handling these infractions. Disciplinary measures must be appropriate for the seriousness of the infraction and in line with the organization's policies and procedures. Depending on the type of infraction, the consequences could be anything from verbal warnings or retraining to suspension or termination.

Ensuring equitable and open application of disciplinary procedures is crucial. Workers must be allowed to comment and explain the disciplinary action. Enforcing disciplinary actions consistently discourages future infractions and strengthens the organization's commitment to compliance.

The organization might have to notify law enforcement, regulatory organizations, or other external authorities about the incident, depending on the type of infraction. To meet legal requirements and show the organization's dedication to accountability and transparency, timely and accurate reporting is crucial.

For instance, financial institutions must notify the Securities and Exchange Commission (SEC) or the Financial Industry Regulatory Authority (FINRA) of material regulatory violations. In a data breach, healthcare organizations might be required to notify the Department of Health and Human Services (HHS) or other pertinent entities. Proper documentation and adherence to reporting standards are essential to reduce legal risks and preserve regulatory compliance.

When addressing compliance infractions, effective communication is essential. The business must maintain open lines of communication with all relevant parties, such as staff members, clients, and investors, regarding the specifics of the violation, the steps taken to rectify it, and the steps taken to ensure that it doesn't happen again. Open communication supports the upkeep of trust, demonstrates accountability, and reassures stakeholders of the organization's dedication to moral behavior and legal compliance.

Organizations should also give regular reports on the progress of repair and corrective action initiatives. This covers informing others about any modifications to the policies or procedures, new training programs, and enhanced internal controls. Frequent updates reaffirm the organization's dedication to ongoing improvement and keep stakeholders informed.

Resolving infractions of compliance allows firms to grow their compliance systems by taking lessons from past mistakes. The company should conduct a post-incident review following a violation to determine lessons learned and assess the efficacy of the reaction. To strengthen the organization's overall compliance posture, this assessment should include determining areas for improvement, evaluating the compliance framework's suitability, and implementing improvements.

As a result of handling compliance infractions, continuous improvement entails improving training programs, reinforcing internal controls, and changing policies and procedures. Organizations may lessen the possibility of future infractions, better predict and handle possible hazards, and promote an ethical culture by taking a proactive approach to compliance management.

To sum up, managing compliance infractions is essential to maintaining a successful compliance program and ensuring a company complies with all applicable laws and regulations. Organizations can effectively resolve issues and prevent future occurrences by recognizing and reporting infractions promptly, conducting comprehensive investigations, putting corrective actions into place, and executing disciplinary penalties. Managing compliance risks and developing a strong compliance culture need open communication, prompt reporting, and an emphasis on ongoing improvement. These endeavors allow establishments to maintain moral principles, protect their standing, and attain sustained prosperity.

Leveraging External Expertise

Using outside expertise is smart for companies looking to improve their compliance systems, handle unique difficulties, and traverse intricate regulatory environments. Organizations can greatly benefit from the abundance of knowledge, expertise, and objectivity that external experts bring regarding managing compliance risks, putting best practices into practice, and meeting regulatory goals. This section examines the benefits of enlisting outside expertise, the kinds of outside experts that are frequently used, and the best ways to incorporate their knowledge into organizational procedures.

External expertise's many important benefits can strengthen an organization's compliance efforts. First, outside specialists offer knowledge and experience that might need to be present within the organization. Regulations about compliance are frequently intricate and dynamic, necessitating in-depth expertise in particular fields. Auditors, legal counsel, and external consultants provide the knowledge and current understanding necessary to handle complex regulatory matters and offer wise counsel.

Second, outside specialists provide an unbiased viewpoint that organizations can use to recognize and resolve possible vulnerabilities or blind spots. Internal teams could be too familiar with particular procedures or methods to see potential problems with objectivity. Outside specialists offer an unbiased evaluation free from personal prejudices and can bring new perspectives on areas that require development.

Employing outside experts also gives firms access to resources and competencies that they might need help to develop internally. For a given regulatory difficulty, hiring a professional compliance consultant may be less expensive than assembling an internal team with the same degree of experience. Adding cutting-edge techniques, technologies, and best practices by external specialists can improve the efficacy of compliance initiatives.

Businesses can work with various outside specialists to handle multiple compliance-related issues. Compliance consultants offer expert counsel and direction on risk management, best practices, and regulatory matters. They can assist companies in conducting gap analysis, creating strategies for meeting particular regulatory needs and designing and implementing compliance programs. Consultants can provide customized solutions because of their vast experience and frequently possess industry-specific knowledge.

Legal specialists must manage legal risks, ensure compliance with relevant laws, and interpret and navigate complicated rules. In addition to drafting and reviewing contracts and representing the company in legal matters or regulatory inquiries, legal advisors can offer legal advice. Their knowledge is crucial for comprehending the legal ramifications of compliance choices and ensuring the company's procedures comply with the law.

External auditors conduct Independent evaluations of an organization's adherence to internal and external policies. They conduct audits to assess the efficiency of internal controls, spot possible non-compliance areas and offer suggestions for enhancement. External audits assist organizations in addressing any shortcomings found throughout the audit process and provide an unbiased evaluation of compliance methods.

Industry-specific specialists contribute an extensive understanding of the best practices and legal requirements unique to a given industry. For instance, experts In healthcare, finance, or environmental regulations can shed light on issues unique to their business and advise on how to comply with rules. Organizations can benefit from the knowledge of industry experts regarding developments and trends impacting their industry.

Careful preparation and coordination are necessary for an organization's compliance initiatives to include outside expertise successfully. Important tactics consist of:

Clearly state the goals and parameters of bringing in outside experts. This entails determining the precise fields —risk management, internal audits, and regulatory compliance—requiring outside expertise. It is easier to ensure outside experts know the company's demands and can offer focused support when these objectives are communicated clearly.

Select outside specialists according to their credentials, background, and suitability for the organization's requirements. Assess their performance history, level of industry experience, and standing to make sure they possess the knowledge and expertise needed to handle the particular difficulties the company is facing. Case studies and references can shed light on an expert's track record of accomplishment.

For their involvement, keep lines of communication open and transparent with outside specialists. Frequent meetings, feedback sessions, and updates make sure that outside specialists continue to support the goals of the company and offer pertinent guidance on time— additionally, good communication aids in resolving any problems or worries that can come up during the interaction.

Integrate the advice and insights from outside specialists into the company's compliance procedures. This could entail implementing new controls, changing policies and procedures, or modifying compliance plans with the expert's advice. Ensure that suggestions are included in the frameworks already in place and that pertinent parties are updated on any modifications.

Keep an eye on how outside knowledge affects the company's compliance initiatives. Assess how well the guidelines worked, how the recommendations were implemented, and how the compliance performance improved overall. This evaluation offers insights into areas where additional support could be required and aids in determining the value of outside expertise.

Developing enduring connections with outside specialists can offer continuing assistance and direction. Consider forming alliances with consultants, attorneys, or business specialists who can provide ongoing support and keep up with changing legal and regulatory requirements. Long-term partnerships enable proactive planning and assist companies in staying ahead of regulatory issues.

Although there are many advantages to using outside knowledge, companies should be aware of potential risks. Among them are:

Because hiring outside specialists can be costly, businesses should consider the services' cost-benefit ratio carefully. It's critical to consider the advantages and disadvantages of not properly resolving compliance issues while weighing the expense of outside expertise.

An excessive reliance on outside specialists could result in a lack of internal knowledge and experience. Organizations must balance internal training and development and external support to provide personnel with the necessary skills and knowledge for continuous compliance management.

Regarding methods or viewpoints, external experts could differ from internal teams. Effective integration of recommendations necessitates clear communication and teamwork to ensure alignment between external instructions and internal practices.

In summary, improving compliance systems, handling regulatory issues, and controlling specific risks can all be accomplished by utilizing outside expertise. Organizations can obtain specialized knowledge, gain objective views, and enhance their compliance operations by enlisting the services of consultants, legal advisers, auditors, and industry specialists. Establishing goals, choosing the appropriate specialists, keeping lines of communication open, and implementing suggestions into organizational procedures are all necessary to integrate outside expertise effectively. Organizations can improve compliance programs, reduce risks, and accomplish regulatory goals by strategically utilizing outside expertise.

Integrating Compliance into Corporate Culture

For businesses to maintain an ethical workplace culture and comply with legal and regulatory standards, compliance must be ingrained into corporate culture. Compliance permeates every facet of an organization's operations when it is made a central feature of the corporate culture, impacting decision-making procedures, actions, and mindsets. This section examines the advantages of developing a compliance-oriented culture, the significance of incorporating compliance into company culture, and the methods for doing so.

Business cultures must incorporate compliance for multiple reasons. First off, a robust culture of compliance reduces legal and regulatory risks. Employee understanding and adherence to regulatory standards increase when compliance is deeply rooted in the organization's beliefs and practices, decreasing the probability of violations and the corresponding fines. Transparency and accountability, which are essential for preserving the organization's standing and stakeholders' trust, are also promoted by an efficient compliance culture.

A compliance-oriented culture improves second moral behavior and judgment. Employees are motivated to behave honorably and make choices consistent with ethical and legal obligations when compliance is ingrained in the company culture. This lowers the possibility of unethical behavior and fosters a supportive workplace where staff members are comfortable voicing concerns and disclosing wrongdoing.

Lastly, incorporating compliance into business culture promotes success and sustainability over the long run. Firms possessing a robust compliance culture are more adept at managing regulatory modifications, accommodating novel demands, and upholding optimal operational efficiency. Organizations may develop a resilient and adaptive workforce capable of handling changing circumstances and taking advantage of new opportunities by prioritizing compliance.

Organizations should employ the following tactics to incorporate compliance into corporate culture effectively.

Integrating compliance into business culture requires a strong commitment from the leadership. Senior managers and executives must show that they are firmly committed to compliance by establishing moral behavior and leading by example. This entails being actively involved in compliance campaigns, emphasizing the value of compliance, and holding oneself and others responsible for following rules and guidelines. The organization's leadership upholds compliance, highlighting its importance and motivating staff to prioritize ethical behavior.

Integrating compliance into business culture requires developing and disseminating clear policies and processes. Policies should specify the organization's standards for moral conduct, adherence to laws, and reporting procedures. Procedures should offer direction on how to carry out and abide by these policies. Making sure that policies and procedures are readily available and updated regularly aids in educating staff members about their obligations and the repercussions of breaking them.

Reinforcing compliance as a component of company culture is largely accomplished through training and education. Regular training sessions covering pertinent rules, compliance requirements, and ethical standards should be offered by organizations. Interactive training sessions customized to meet the unique requirements of various departments or positions are ideal. Organizations may provide staff with the necessary information and skills to effectively handle compliance difficulties by investing in thorough training.

Creating an environment where communication is open is essential to developing a compliance-oriented culture. It should be easy for staff members to voice concerns, pose inquiries, and get advice on compliance-related issues. Whistleblower hotlines are one type of anonymous reporting mechanism organizations might set up to enable employees to voice concerns without worrying about consequences. Clear lines of communication foster an environment of openness and trust while assisting in the early resolution of possible compliance problems.

Compliance's significance within the business culture is reinforced by integrating it into performance management and award programs. Employers should recognize staff members dedicated to moral conduct and legal compliance by rewarding them and incorporating compliance-related factors into performance reviews. Acknowledging and applauding compliance accomplishments motivates staff to prioritize compliance in everyday tasks and promotes positive behavior.

Regular monitoring and assessment are necessary to determine whether compliance integration initiatives are effective. Periodic inspections of compliance processes, policies, and training programs are recommended for organizations to identify areas that require improvement. This entails assessing how compliance activities affect performance, employee behavior, and organizational culture. Organizations can improve their compliance culture by making the required adjustments with the support of routine monitoring, which helps guarantee that compliance stays a top priority.

It is ensured that regulatory considerations are incorporated into business decisions by integrating compliance into decision-making processes. This entails integrating evaluations and compliance checks into operational procedures, strategic efforts, and project planning. Organizations can proactively manage potential risks and guarantee that their operations are by legal and ethical standards by considering compliance consequences during the decision-making process.

Establishing a culture focused on compliance has many advantages for businesses. Organizations with a strong compliance culture are better able to detect and manage regulatory risks, lowering the chance of infractions and the resulting penalties. Organizations can retain operational continuity and avoid expensive legal challenges by proactively addressing compliance issues.

Customers, investors, and regulators are among the stakeholders more inclined to respect and trust an organization dedicated to ethical behavior and compliance. A good reputation raises the organization's credibility, opens more commercial options, and forges closer bonds with stakeholders.

Workers are more likely to feel appreciated and supported in a compliance-oriented culture. Increased employee engagement, contentment, and retention result from a pleasant work environment that places a high value on moral behavior and honest communication.

Integrating compliance into corporate culture promotes operational excellence by guaranteeing that procedures and policies align with legal standards and industry best practices. As a result, operations become more effective and efficient, errors are decreased, and performance is enhanced overall.

To sum up, companies must incorporate compliance into their corporate culture to ensure they follow legal and regulatory standards and promote moral behavior and decision-making. Organizations can develop a strong compliance culture and integrate compliance into daily operations by putting techniques like performance management, open communication, training and education, leadership commitment, clear policies, and regular monitoring into practice. Higher risk management, higher employee engagement, enhanced reputation, and operational excellence are all advantages of a compliance-oriented culture. Organizations can develop a strong, moral workforce that promotes sustainability and long-term success by prioritizing compliance.

CHAPTER V

Responding to Regulatory Changes

Proactive vs. Reactive Approaches to Compliance

A key component of organizational governance is compliance management, which ensures that a company complies with internal policies, laws, and regulations. Companies can handle compliance in two ways: proactively or reactively. Each has advantages and disadvantages of its own. The distinctions between proactive and reactive methods of compliance are examined in this section, along with how they affect long-term success, risk management, and organizational performance.

Anticipating and resolving compliance concerns before they become real is a proactive approach to compliance. This proactive approach concentrates on averting problems by putting preventive measures in place and consistently enhancing compliance procedures—the fundamental components of a proactive strategy.

Proactive organizations conduct extensive risk assessments to detect possible compliance problems before they materialize. Identifying potential risk areas entails examining corporate procedures, market trends, and regulatory needs. Organizations can create and implement plans to reduce risks and stop violations by seeing possible problems early on.

Organizations that take the initiative spend money creating thorough rules and processes that comply with legal standards and industry best practices. These guidelines are intended to direct staff members in adhering to regulations and resolving possible problems. Proactive companies also ensure that staff members know compliance rules and how to apply them in their duties by offering frequent training and education.

Proactive compliance strategies require regular audits and monitoring. Companies use routine monitoring systems to monitor compliance performance, spot policy violations, and handle possible problems before they get out of hand. Audits are conducted to determine what needs improvement and assess how well compliance programs work. Organizations may stay ahead of possible hazards and ensure compliance procedures are successful by implementing ongoing monitoring and auditing.

A proactive strategy emphasizes continuous improvement by routinely evaluating and revising compliance procedures in light of new risks, regulatory changes, and input from monitoring and audits. Businesses are dedicated to improving compliance initiatives and changing to meet evolving needs. The constant improvement of compliance procedures is guaranteed by this iterative method.

A reactive approach to compliance, on the other hand, focuses on fixing compliance problems after they arise. This strategy is on reacting to infractions or breaches of the law as soon as they are discovered. The following are the main traits of a reactive approach.

Reactive organizations usually address compliance problems as soon as they appear. This includes handling infractions, overseeing regulatory inquiries, and carrying out post-mortem remedial measures. The main priorities are to minimize the problem's immediate effects and find a quick solution.

When handling compliance violations, reactive businesses prioritize crisis management and damage control. This could entail handling legal repercussions, maintaining public relations, and repairing any harm to one's reputation. Prioritizing reducing the adverse effects of the infraction and promptly returning to regular operations is the main goal.

Preventive actions should be given more weight in a reactive strategy. Organizations might not take proactive measures to stop future infractions, instead addressing compliance issues only after they arise. This may lead to persistent difficulties and a cycle of reactive problem-solving.

Reactive organizations run the risk of not complying with regulations, which can result in fines, penalties, or legal repercussions. In addition to the potential financial burden of handling regulatory investigations and dealing with infractions, the organization may suffer from a damaged reputation and a decline in stakeholder trust.

A comparison of proactive and reactive strategies reveals the advantages and difficulties of each tactic.

Regarding risk management, a proactive approach to compliance usually works better. Organizations can manage risks and lower the probability of violations by foreseeing future difficulties and putting preventative measures before they become more serious. Reactive approaches, however, frequently entail dealing with problems after they've already happened, which could lead to higher expenses and more risk exposure.

In the long run, proactive compliance measures are more economical. Organizations can avoid expensive infractions and fines from the government by investing in training, preventive measures, and ongoing development. While putting preventative tactics into practice may have upfront costs, these expenditures can pay off in the long run by lowering risk and producing savings. Conversely, reactive strategies could result in greater expenses for handling infractions, handling emergencies, and paying fines related to regulations.

A proactive strategy fosters an organization's culture of compliance and moral behavior. Workers are urged to follow rules, be aware of their obligations, and support an environment that strives for constant development. On the other hand, a reactive strategy could foster a crisis management culture in which compliance is only addressed when issues arise. Employees may need to be more attentive and place more value on preventive measures.

Businesses that take a proactive stance will likely succeed in the long run. These companies can adjust to regulatory changes, manage new risks, and uphold their good reputations by incorporating compliance into their strategic planning and constant practice improvement. Persistent compliance concerns, legal battles, and reputational harm may impact reactive firms' long-term health and expansion.

Reactive approach components can be usefully incorporated into an organization's overall compliance strategy, even if proactive approaches are often preferred for their advantages in risk management and cost-effectiveness. Strong incident response plans and crisis management procedures, for instance, can support preventative efforts and guarantee that the company is ready to handle compliance issues should they emerge.

To sum up, companies must incorporate compliance into their corporate culture to ensure they follow legal and regulatory standards and promote moral behavior and decision-making. Organizations can develop a strong compliance culture and integrate compliance into daily operations by putting techniques like performance management, open communication, training and education, leadership commitment, clear policies, and regular monitoring into practice. Higher risk management, higher employee engagement, enhanced reputation, and operational excellence are all advantages of a compliance-oriented culture. Organizations can develop a strong, moral workforce that promotes sustainability and long-term success by prioritizing compliance.

Change Management in Regulatory Compliance

Change management is crucial to regulatory compliance, especially in a setting where rules and laws are constantly changing. Organizations implementing effective change management can better maintain compliance, adjust to regulation changes, and reduce non-compliance risks. This section examines the benefits of an organized strategy for responding to regulatory updates, the role of change management in regulatory compliance, and important change management techniques.

Organizations must constantly adapt to new laws, rules, and industry norms to maintain regulatory compliance. Change management becomes crucial to maintaining current and efficient compliance procedures. Organizations run the danger of non-compliance, which can result in fines, financial losses, and reputational harm if they systematically manage regulatory changes.

Planning, carrying out, and overseeing modifications to compliance procedures and practices in an organized manner are all part of regulatory compliance change management. It guarantees that the organization continues to comply with regulatory standards and that all stakeholders are educated, taught, and prepared to manage new needs. Instead of responding to compliance concerns as they emerge, organizations may anticipate and address regulatory modifications proactively with the support of a well-managed change process.

Creating an organized framework for change management is essential to successfully managing regulatory changes. This framework should include processes for determining, evaluating, and implementing changes. Important elements of the framework consist of:

It is keeping an eye on new developments in regulations and spotting impending changes that could affect the company. This entails keeping up with regulatory updates, industry groups, and legal counsel regarding new laws, changes, and industry standards.

It assesses how prospective regulatory changes might affect the organization's policies, practices, and operations. This entails examining the change's extent, evaluating its hazards, and determining the resources needed to implement it.

It is creating and carrying out a plan to put the regulation change into effect. This includes revising training materials, updating policies and procedures, and informing stakeholders and staff of changes.

Monitor how well the changes have been executed and make any necessary corrections. This includes conducting follow-up audits, getting staff input, and assessing compliance performance.

Ensuring the seamless implementation of regulatory changes necessitates early stakeholder engagement in the change management process. Department heads, compliance officials, senior management, and legal counsel are important stakeholders. It is beneficial to include these parties in the change process:

Obtain senior leadership and important stakeholders' buy-in and support, essential for successfully implementing change.

Ascertain that all teams and departments know the change and their respective roles and responsibilities in bringing about compliance.

To help ensure a smoother transition and lower the chance of non-compliance, identify and address any opposition or reservations about the change.

Maintaining compliance with new regulatory obligations by employees requires effective communication and training. The following are some training and communication strategies.

Create and provide focused training courses that cover the particular adjustments and how they affect the duties and responsibilities of staff members. Training must be comprehensive, interesting, and suited to various organizational levels.

Inform staff members on regulatory changes and offer continuing support by using a variety of communication channels, including emails, meetings, and intranet updates. Effective and regular communication informs staff members and reaffirms the significance of compliance.

The efficacy of handling regulatory changes can be improved using technology and change management tools. The following are some ways that tools like project management systems, risk assessment frameworks, and compliance management software can speed up the change process.

We are monitoring deadlines and regulatory updates as well as the implementation of changes.

Facilitating cooperation across departments and stakeholders engaged in the change process.

We offer information and analysis to track the effects of modifications and evaluate compliance levels.

There are various advantages to using a structured change management approach for regulatory compliance.

The chance of non-compliance and the fines accompanying it is reduced by actively monitoring regulatory changes. Organizations can prevent major difficulties by avoiding regulatory revisions and addressing possible concerns before they arise.

An organized method simplifies implementing changes, increasing effectiveness and reducing the time and resources needed. This results in less disturbance to business operations and faster adaption to changing requirements.

Maintaining compliance standards is encouraged by ensuring all staff members are taught and informed about new legislation. This lowers the possibility of infractions and improves the organization's overall compliance performance.

Future regulatory changes can be adapted to by organizations more readily when they have a solid change management framework in place. Organizations can enhance their resilience and agility in managing the dynamic regulatory environment by implementing a systematic strategy.

In summary, change management is essential to regulatory compliance since it helps businesses adjust to new rules and regulations. Organizations can effectively handle regulatory changes by implementing a change management framework, including stakeholders, offering training, and employing change management tools. A structured approach has several advantages: decreased risk, more adaptability, increased efficiency, and improved compliance. In a changing regulatory landscape, proactive change management strategies assist firms in preserving compliance, reducing risks, and achieving long-term success.

Stakeholder Communication and Engagement

Stakeholder engagement and communication that works are essential to successful compliance management. Stakeholders are critical to an organization's ability to follow rules and uphold moral principles. They can be anything from workers and clients to investors and regulators. This section examines the advantages of building strong stakeholder relationships, the tactics for effective communication, and the significance of stakeholder engagement and communication in compliance.

For several reasons, stakeholder participation and communication are essential. First, ensuring that all pertinent parties know organizational rules and compliance needs requires clear and regular communication. This guarantees that all parties understand their roles and duties in upholding compliance and helps avoid misunderstandings.

Involving stakeholders also promotes a transparent and trustworthy culture. Stakeholders are more likely to support compliance measures and contribute to a positive company culture when they believe their concerns and suggestions are valued. This assistance can boost overall company performance and increase the efficacy of compliance programs.

Third, proactive problem-solving and risk management are made easier for firms by good stakeholder communication. Organizations can minimize the chance of infractions and related fines by keeping lines of communication open and promptly identifying and resolving compliance issues.

Finding the important stakeholders is the first step in a successful stakeholder communication strategy. Among the stakeholders are:

Board members, management, and employees are considered internal stakeholders.

Community members, investors, suppliers, regulators, and customers.

Organizations may effectively engage with different stakeholder groups and customize their communication methods by thoroughly understanding their requirements, expectations, and concerns.

Developing a thorough communication strategy is necessary to manage the involvement of stakeholders. The plan should include:

Specify communication objectives, such as addressing concerns, gaining feedback, or increasing understanding of compliance requirements.

Craft concise and coherent messaging that effectively communicates crucial details on compliance guidelines, modifications, and anticipated outcomes.

Use relevant channels, such as emails, meetings, reports, or social media, to communicate with various stakeholder groups.

Establish the communication frequency to ensure all parties are informed and updated on time.

To effectively engage stakeholders, companies must communicate in both directions—that is, they must listen to stakeholder feedback and provide it. Among the techniques for encouraging two-way communication are:

Provide avenues for interested parties to offer comments, voice concerns, or pose inquiries. Forums, suggestion boxes, and surveys may be examples of this.

Send out regular updates on compliance-related topics, such as regulatory changes, the status of compliance projects, or audit results. This maintains informed and involved stakeholders.

Arrange conferences, seminars, or webinars to discuss compliance-related topics and get feedback from interested parties. This participatory method promotes engagement and fosters deep conversation.

Diverse stakeholders possess differing degrees of interest and proficiency in compliance-related problems. It is essential to adapt communication to the unique requirements of each audience. This comprises:

When speaking with non-experts, provide compliance information in an intelligible and straightforward manner; stay away from jargon and technical phrases.

Disseminate information pertinent to each stakeholder group, such as updates on investor regulations or employee compliance procedures.

Use channels and formats according to stakeholder preferences, such as written reports, visual presentations, or digital platforms.

Establishing a transparent culture increases involvement and trust among stakeholders. Companies can promote openness by communicating promptly and accurately and being open about the difficulties, developments, and results of compliance.

Give prompt, courteous responses to questions and concerns from stakeholders. This shows a dedication to resolving problems and upholding honest dialogue.

Ensure stakeholders know the organization's dedication to moral conduct and regulatory compliance by holding people and groups accountable for compliance-related actions.

Stakeholder involvement and communication that is effective has various advantages.

It can be guaranteed that compliance obligations are recognized and fulfilled using active stakeholder involvement and clear communication. This improves overall compliance performance and lowers the chance of breaches.

Recognizing and reducing compliance risks early is easier when stakeholder concerns and input are addressed proactively. This can stop problems from worsening and lower the risk of fines or reputational harm.

Establishing solid bonds with stakeholders promotes cooperation and trust. Positive company culture, helpful feedback, and support for compliance measures will likely come from engaged stakeholders.

Good communication upholds the organization's commitment to moral conduct and encourages transparency. Stakeholder confidence in the organization's compliance efforts is increased as a result.

Businesses that communicate effectively with their stakeholders can better handle obstacles and regulation changes. Organizations can better adjust to changing compliance standards by keeping lines of communication open and taking proactive measures to address concerns.

To sum up, successful compliance management necessitates stakeholder participation and communication. Organizations can improve their compliance efforts and cultivate strong relationships with stakeholders by identifying important stakeholders, creating a thorough communication plan, putting two-way communication into practice, customizing messaging to audience needs, and encouraging openness. Stronger relationships, enhanced risk management, increased transparency, improved compliance performance, and more organizational resilience are all advantages of successful stakeholder communication. Setting stakeholder involvement as a top priority aids in an organization's long-term success, risk mitigation, and regulatory compliance. According to stakeholder preferences can be guaranteed recognizing and reducing compliance risks early is easier.

Case Studies of Effective Response Strategies

Sustaining regulatory compliance and safeguarding organizational integrity require effective ways of responding to compliance issues. By analyzing practical instances, entities can get valuable perspectives on efficacious strategies for managing compliance-related matters. This section provides case studies of businesses that have handled compliance issues well, emphasizing their approaches and important lessons learned.

Johnson & Johnson had a serious compliance and crisis management problem in 1982 after seven people in the Chicago area died from Tylenol capsules laced with cyanide. The company's handling of this incident is often used as a model for successful crisis management and regulatory compliance.

With promptitude, Johnson & Johnson removed over 31 million Tylenol bottles from retail shelves and announced a nationwide recall of their goods. This decisive response showed the company's dedication to consumer safety and regulatory compliance.

The business communicated with the public, the media, and the authorities openly and honestly. Regular updates on the recall procedure and the crisis management measures were given by Johnson & Johnson.

Johnson & Johnson investigated the tampering case closely with law police and the FDA. The organization showed a dedication to compliance and public safety by cooperating with regulatory authorities.

Johnson & Johnson introduced tamper-evident packaging for Tylenol and other medications in response to the crisis. By taking preventative action, possible weaknesses were fixed, and product safety was improved.

For compliance problems to be effectively managed, swift decision-making is essential. Johnson & Johnson showed a great commitment to customer safety by promptly recalling some products, which served to lessen the effect of the disaster.

Open communication with stakeholders is crucial during a crisis for managing public perception and fostering trust. To preserve trust and credibility, information and changes must be shared transparently.

Addressing compliance concerns thoroughly and successfully is ensured by strong collaboration with law enforcement and regulatory bodies.

When it was discovered in 2015 that Volkswagen had cheated on emissions tests for diesel vehicles using software, the corporation was confronted with a serious compliance dilemma. The "Dieselgate" controversy had a major impact on the company's reputation and regulatory standing.

Volkswagen expressed regret for its actions and officially acknowledged the problem. The business apologized for the deceit and acknowledged using illicit software.

VW established agreements with governing bodies and impacted customers. The corporation consented to pay billions in fines and compensation to settle legal and financial accusations.

Volkswagen addressed the non-compliance with regulations by implementing significant internal adjustments. This involved reorganizing its legal and compliance departments, improving internal controls, and creating new policies and processes to stop such infractions.

Volkswagen responded by pledging to fund the development of electric cars and environmentally friendly technologies. This strategic change aimed to comply with market and regulatory requirements while repairing the company's reputation.

Rebuilding credibility and confidence requires accepting responsibility for compliance errors and publicly admitting them. Admitting faults and pledging to make amends transparently shows accountability.

Resolving compliance issues and minimizing reputational harm can be accomplished by addressing the legal and financial ramifications through settlements and compensation.

Adopting internal improvements and fortifying compliance systems are essential to averting future infractions and guaranteeing sustained conformity to regulations.

The Wells Fargo Scandal Involving False Accounts. A controversy surrounding the creation of fictitious client accounts at Wells Fargo to hit sales targets surfaced in 2016. Significant regulatory attention and reputational harm to the corporation resulted from the problem.

In response to the incident, Wells Fargo changed its leadership and held people accountable. The organization fired those engaged in the fraud and brought in fresh leadership to promote change.

In addition to attempting to address issues, Wells Fargo set up a compensation fund for impacted clients. The business aimed to compensate consumers and offer apologies for the illegal accounts.

To avoid such problems in the future, the company implemented new internal controls and compliance measures. This involved tweaks to sales procedures, increased education initiatives, and strengthened supervision systems.

Publicly apologizing, Wells Fargo expressed its resolve to resolve the problems and enhance its procedures. The organization endeavored to reestablish confidence with its clientele and interested parties using open dialogue and remedial measures.

Demonstrating a commitment to addressing compliance breaches and promoting organizational transformation necessitates holding people accountable and implementing leadership changes.

Giving impacted customers compensation lessens the impact of compliance lapses and helps rebuild customer confidence.

Strengthening compliance procedures and internal controls is crucial to ensure regulatory conformance and prevent future problems.

Millions of consumers' personal and financial information were stolen in a significant data breach at Target in 2013. As a result, the business came under intense regulatory scrutiny and suffered harm to its brand.

Target provided free credit monitoring services and swiftly informed impacted customers. The business swiftly notified clients of the security incident and helped.

To identify the source of the breach and put corrective measures in place, Target carried out a comprehensive investigation. The organization collaborated with cybersecurity specialists to improve its data security procedures and stop further intrusions.

Target supplied information regarding the breach and its reaction and assisted regulatory bodies. The business tried to abide by data protection laws and handle regulatory issues.

Target used PR campaigns to repair its image and win customers' trust. Among these were advertising initiatives emphasizing the business's dedication to security and client safety.

Managing the effects of a data breach and preserving consumer trust depend on promptly informing impacted customers and offering assistance.

A thorough investigation and remedial methods must be implemented to address the core reasons for a breach and enhance security.

To handle regulatory scrutiny and show a commitment to data protection, cooperation with regulatory authorities and addressing compliance concerns are helpful.

In conclusion, prompt action, accountability, openness, and proactive actions are essential to successful compliance response methods. Companies can effectively handle compliance crises by identifying problems, taking corrective action, and interacting with stakeholders, as demonstrated by the case studies of Johnson & Johnson, Volkswagen, Wells Fargo, and Target. Organizations can create strong reaction plans to handle regulatory obstacles and uphold compliance by taking note of these instances.

Tools and Resources for Staying Update

Organizations must be informed about regulatory changes to maintain compliance and minimize legal and financial risks. Laws and rules are always changing, creating a dynamic regulatory environment. Companies need to use a range of tools and resources to address these developments and ensure compliance. This section examines the most important instruments and sources for being current on regulatory changes and their function in maintaining compliance.

Software for regulatory compliance is made to assist businesses in monitoring, controlling, and reacting to regulation changes. These instruments provide attributes.

Software for compliance can keep track of changes to regulations in various industries and jurisdictions. By doing this, firms can remain up to speed on new and revised regulations affecting their operations.

Policies, procedures, and regulatory filings are just a few examples of papers that organizations can keep and arrange according to compliance with document management tools included in the software.

Real-time alerts and notifications regarding regulatory changes are a feature of many compliance tools, enabling firms to handle new requirements swiftly.

Audit and reporting features are frequently included in compliance software, which aids businesses in monitoring their compliance status and producing reports for internal and external stakeholders.

In the market, well-liked options include SAI Global's Compliance 360, Wolters Kluwer's OneSumX, and Thomson Reuters' Regulatory Intelligence.

To stay informed about changes to regulations and industry standards, professional regulatory agencies and industry associations are invaluable resources. These groups offer:

Regulatory authorities frequently publish updates, guidance, and interpretations of new regulations. By signing up for these bodies' newsletters or alerts, organizations can be guaranteed to get information promptly.

Numerous associations provide conferences, webinars, and training sessions on best practices for compliance and regulation changes.

Professional associations offer chances to network with regulators, specialists, and colleagues. Interacting with these networks can reveal information about new regulations and trends in the market.

Notable organizations that provide information for staying educated are the Financial Industry Regulatory Authority (FINRA), the International Compliance Association (ICA), and the American Bar Association (ABA).

Government websites and regulatory portals are the main places to find information about new and revised regulations. Among these resources are:

Official texts of new laws, modifications, and regulations are frequently posted on government websites. These publications offer reliable information about what is required by rules.

Numerous governments keep online databases that allow firms to look up and obtain recommendations, regulations, and other compliance information.

Certain government websites allow subscribers to receive notifications and updates regarding regulatory changes pertinent to particular sectors or industries.

Important government resources include the UK's legislation.gov.uk, the European Union's EUR-Lex portal, and the United States Federal Register.

Legal and compliance consultancy services provide expert advice on managing compliance and negotiating regulatory changes. These offerings offer:

Law firms and compliance consultants provide legal analysis and interpretations of the legislation to help enterprises comprehend the consequences of new regulations and the necessary steps to comply with them.

To evaluate an organization's compliance with existing regulations and pinpoint possibilities for development, advisory services can carry out compliance audits.

Professionals can help with the creation and execution of risk management plans and compliance initiatives, among other regulatory strategies.

Both specialized compliance consultancies like Protiviti and BAE Systems and large legal firms like Baker McKenzie, Dentons, and Hogan Lovells offer these services.

Updates on regulatory changes and new trends can be found in industry news channels and publications. Among these resources are:

Industry publications and trade newspapers offer in-depth reporting on regulatory developments and how they affect particular industries.

Articles, analyses, and comments on current regulatory changes and compliance challenges are frequently found on news websites and online platforms.

Organizations that conduct industry research provide whitepapers and reports on regulatory trends, providing insightful analysis and projections.

To keep up with the latest developments in regulation, one might consult publications like Compliance Week, Law360, and the Corporate Governance blog of the Harvard Law School.

Programs for professional development and training are crucial for keeping compliance personnel informed about changes in regulations. These courses provide:

Workshops and seminars offer real-world experience and useful advice on handling regulatory compliance and adjusting to new regulations.

Compliance professionals can improve their skills and knowledge by enrolling in certification programs that provide specialized compliance and regulatory topics training.

Professionals can stay current on their schedules by taking advantage of online learning platforms' flexible training alternatives on regulatory subjects.

Various training and certification programs are available from the International Compliance Association (ICA), the Compliance Certification Board (CCB), and Coursera.

Automated monitoring and intelligence systems use technology to monitor and evaluate regulation changes.

Automated systems constantly monitor regulatory sources and notify the organization in real-time of any pertinent changes.

Organizations can evaluate the effects of regulatory changes and make data-driven decisions by utilizing advanced analytics capabilities.

These solutions help expedite updating policies and procedures by integrating with current compliance management systems.

Comply Advantage and Risk Watch are two RegTech products that provide automated monitoring and intelligence for regulatory compliance.

In conclusion, using various methods and resources is necessary to stay informed about regulatory developments. Organizations can stay informed and compliant by using regulatory compliance software, professional regulatory bodies, government websites, legal and compliance advice services, industry news, professional development programs, and automated monitoring technologies, among other resources. Organizations may manage compliance risks, navigate the complicated regulatory landscape, and preserve operational integrity by appropriately using these resources.

CHAPTER VI

Legal and Ethical Considerations

Legal Obligations vs. Ethical Responsibilities

Individuals and organizations alike must recognize the difference between ethical and legal responsibilities. Although both ideas are crucial for directing actions and choices, they have various applications and functions in different domains. This section examines the distinctions between ethical and legal responsibilities, how they interact, and what this means for corporate behavior and compliance.

Requirements set forth by governmental laws and regulations are known as legal responsibilities. These duties, intended to preserve law and order, safeguard rights, and guarantee equitable behavior, are enforced legally.

Regulations, case law, and statutes codify legal responsibilities. Their definition is unambiguous, precise, and enshrined in legal documents, offering a guide for proper conduct.

Penalties under the law may include fines, imprisonment, or other sanctions for breaking duties. Courts, other legal institutions, and regulatory organizations all carry out legal enforcement.

Legal obligations cannot be subjectively interpreted; they are objective. Adherence to recognized legal standards is the basis for assessing compliance.

To stay out of trouble legally and preserve their operational validity, both individuals and organizations must abide by their legal commitments. An essential component of corporate governance and operations is legal compliance.

Labor laws are regulations that control employees' rights, pay, and working conditions. Rules about waste control and environmental preservation. Guidelines for accounting procedures and financial disclosures.

On the other hand, ethical obligations relate to moral standards and ideals that direct conduct above and beyond what the law requires. Although not required by law, ethical commitments are crucial for developing integrity, trust, and healthy relationships.

Moral precepts include justice, decency, and respect serve as the foundation for ethical obligations. Conventions related to culture, society, and the workplace frequently influence them.

Even if moral obligations cannot be enforced by law, upholding moral principles is essential to building trust with stakeholders and preserving one's good reputation.

Subjective in nature, ethical obligations can change depending on cultural norms, corporate culture, and personal convictions. Balancing conflicting ideals and interests is a common step in making moral decisions.

A favorable business culture, strengthened relationships, and increased credibility are all benefits of ethical behavior that lead to long-term success.

I am giving stakeholders and customers accurate and transparent information. It goes above and beyond the call of duty to implement actions that improve the environment and society.

Ensuring workers receive fair treatment and refraining from prejudice or partiality.

Even though they are separate, moral and legal obligations frequently overlap and impact one another.

Comprehending their mutual influence is crucial for efficient adherence and ethical behavior.

While ethical responsibilities frequently reflect higher levels of conduct, legal obligations indicate the minimal standards imposed by law. Even if an organization complies with the law, it may not uphold ethical standards. For example, even while a business complies with environmental standards, it may face criticism for failing to implement more sustainable practices.

Promoting responsible behavior can benefit from the combined influence of legal and ethical factors. Respecting legal requirements as well as moral standards aids in an organization's long-term development, reputation building, and cultivation of stakeholder confidence.

When moral duties and legal obligations disagree, conflicts may result. Organizations in these situations must carefully balance these conflicts, frequently giving ethical concerns precedence over legal requirements. For instance, to safeguard its workers and maintain its moral principles, a business may adopt stricter safety regulations than those mandated by law.

Laws and regulations can be developed with ethical considerations in mind. Companies with a strong ethical leadership culture can help to shape industry regulations and provide higher standards.

For enterprises, it is crucial to comprehend and strike a balance between legal and ethical commitments. Important ramifications consist of the following:

Businesses that respect moral and legal obligations can better establish and preserve a good reputation. Organizations that exhibit ethical behavior gain credibility, fortify their connections with stakeholders, and set themselves apart from competitors.

Respecting legal requirements reduces the possibility of fines and enforcement proceedings. Taking care of ethical obligations simultaneously lowers reputational risks and promotes a pleasant workplace culture.

Legal and ethical issues should be taken into account by organizations when making decisions. Ensuring consistent and responsible behavior is facilitated by developing rules and procedures representing legal compliance and moral ideals.

Employee behavior must be guided by training on ethical and legal norms to foster a culture of integrity and compliance.

In summary, moral and legal responsibilities play distinct but complementary roles in directing actions and choices. Legal responsibilities are ethical standards and ideals that direct behavior above and above the minimum criteria set forth by law, whereas legal obligations are enforceable requirements imposed by law. Organizations must comprehend how legal and ethical factors interact to manage compliance, foster trust, and achieve long-term success. Organizations can cultivate a culture of integrity, improve their reputation, and benefit society by balancing legal responsibilities and moral ambitions.

Balancing Business Goals with Compliance

For companies looking to accomplish their goals while abiding by legal and regulatory obligations, striking a balance between business goals and compliance is crucial. If this balance is managed well, businesses can pursue growth and profitability without sacrificing moral principles or legal requirements. The main ideas of balancing compliance and company objectives are examined in this section, along with some helpful tactics and difficult situations.

A business's aims might be anything from raising revenue, gaining market share, improving customer happiness, and promoting innovation. Contrarily, compliance entails abiding by the rules, laws, and guidelines controlling businesses' operations. These rules address data privacy, labor rights, environmental protection, and financial reporting.

For several reasons, balancing compliance and business objectives is crucial. Legal ramifications, monetary losses, and reputational harm are all possible outcomes of noncompliance. Firms may effectively manage risks and avoid potential hazards by integrating compliance into business plans.

By ensuring that companies follow the law, compliance helps to promote sustainable growth. While pursuing ambitious corporate objectives may result in short-term gains, it may also endanger long-term success.

Respecting compliance guidelines contributes to developing trust among stakeholders, partners, and consumers. A good reputation for integrity and ethical behavior fosters positive relationships and increases corporate credibility.

Businesses can use a variety of tactics to strike a balance between compliance and business objectives successfully:

Compliance should be viewed as an independent role rather than as part of the main business plan. Organizations can ensure regulatory requirements are considered in decision-making by coordinating compliance goals with business objectives.

Organizations can more successfully manage their regulatory duties by implementing thorough compliance programs. To guarantee compliance with legal requirements, these programs must incorporate policies, processes, training, and oversight methods.

Fostering a culture of compliance within the company encourages moral conduct and conformity to regulations. Establishing a commitment to compliance and motivating staff to give ethical issues top priority are two ways that leadership should set the tone.

Efficiency may be increased, and compliance procedures streamlined by utilizing technology and compliance management systems. Organizations can efficiently handle regulatory obligations using tools like risk management software, data analytics, and automated compliance monitoring.

Involving stakeholders, including partners, consumers, and staff, balances corporate objectives and compliance. Identifying any compliance concerns and taking proactive measures to rectify them can be facilitated by transparent communication and engagement with stakeholders.

Achieving compliance while balancing corporate goals comes with several challenges.

Complying with regulations can be challenging for firms due to its complexity and variation across various industries and jurisdictions. Maintaining compliance in this regulatory environment calls for constant observation and adjustment.

There may be conflicts between business objectives and compliance standards. Adopting ambitious growth methods, for instance, may pressure one to eschew regulations or take shortcuts. Companies must figure out how to balance these competing goals without sacrificing compliance.

Program implementation and upkeep for compliance might demand a lot of resources. Businesses may need help to devote enough resources to compliance tasks while still achieving their objectives.

Organizations must be informed about regulation changes to maintain compliance, as they are always changing. Flexibility might be difficult and demanding when simultaneously pursuing corporate goals and new rules.

Organizations can use the following best practices to help them deal with the difficulties of balancing compliance and commercial goals.

Frequent risk assessments assist in identifying possible compliance concerns and how they may affect organizational objectives. Organizations can create strategies to manage risks and match compliance efforts with business goals by conducting proactive risk assessments.

Integrating compliance into business processes is easier by having clear governance structures, such as oversight committees and specialized compliance teams. Governance frameworks facilitate effective accountability and decision-making.

Employee awareness and comprehension of regulatory standards must be maintained via ongoing compliance-related training and development. Employees who receive continuing education can better make judgments supporting regulatory requirements and corporate objectives.

Staff members can voice concerns and report any infractions by establishing reporting procedures for compliance-related issues. Resolving compliance issues early on is facilitated by efficient reporting systems.

Policies and procedures for compliance can be kept current and useful by routinely examining and revising them. Maintaining alignment and addressing new issues is facilitated by updating policies to consider modifications to laws and corporate objectives.

An essential component of good organizational management is balancing compliance and business objectives. Organizations can accomplish goals while abiding by legal and regulatory obligations by incorporating compliance into corporate strategy, creating strong compliance processes, cultivating a compliance culture, utilizing technology, and involving stakeholders. Organizations can effectively navigate the challenges of a complex regulatory landscape, competing goals, limited resources, and dynamic regulations by implementing best practices like regular risk assessments, well-defined governance structures, ongoing training, efficient reporting mechanisms, and policy reviews. Ultimately, a balanced approach to compliance and business objectives promotes risk management, long-term growth, and a favorable reputation—all of which help companies prosper in a regulated and competitive landscape.

Corporate Social Responsibility and Compliance

Compliance and corporate social responsibility (CSR) are closely linked and significantly impact an organization's operating procedures, moral standards, and reputation. Complying with legal and regulatory obligations is the main focus of compliance, but corporate social responsibility (CSR) involves a wider commitment to ethical practices, social impact, and environmental stewardship. This section examines the connection between compliance and corporate social responsibility (CSR), their importance, and how businesses can successfully combine both to meet legal requirements and have a positive social impact.

The term "corporate social responsibility" describes companies' voluntarily undertaken measures to contribute to society in addition to their legal duties. CSR includes various projects and activities to resolve economic, social, and environmental problems. Important facets of CSR comprise.

CSR programs seek to advance social concerns, strengthen employee welfare, and boost community well-being. This can involve charitable giving, participating in the community, and working to remove social injustices.

CSR includes actions that reduce their negative effects on the environment and advance sustainability. Businesses may cut waste, conserve the environment, and put energy-saving measures into place.

CSR reflects a company's dedication to moral conduct in its operations. Fair labor standards, ethical sourcing, and open communication with stakeholders are all part of this.

One of the most important aspects of CSR is interacting with stakeholders, such as clients, staff members, and investors. Organizations aim to comprehend and attend to the expectations and concerns of their stakeholders.

CSR and compliance are complementary facets of ethical company operations. While compliance is concerned with following the law, corporate social responsibility (CSR) goes beyond the letter of the law to cover more general ethical and social duties.

The legal framework for CSR projects is provided by compliance. Before organizations pursue further social and environmental aims, they must comply with regulatory restrictions.

Credibility and reliability are enhanced by an organization's effective adherence to laws and regulations. This helps CSR initiatives solidify the company's reputation as a trustworthy and moral enterprise.

Organizations can manage legal and regulatory risks by adhering to compliance. Organizations can prevent legal problems that jeopardize their brand and CSR programs by following the law.

By incorporating compliance with CSR plans, organizations can better connect their goals with ethical and legal constraints. This alignment guarantees that a solid basis of legal compliance supports CSR initiatives.

There are various techniques that organizations can implement to integrate compliance with CSR successfully. Ensuring consistency and alignment can be facilitated by developing comprehensive policies covering compliance and CSR objectives. Legal obligations, moral principles, and social responsibility pledges should all be outlined in policies.

Effective management and accountability are ensured by establishing governance structures that supervise compliance and CSR initiatives. CSR teams, compliance officers, and specialized committees may be examples.

Employees are encouraged to prioritize ethical behavior and social effects by fostering a culture prioritizing compliance and CSR. Leadership is essential to establish the tone and emphasize the significance of both elements.

Organizations can evaluate their effectiveness and pinpoint opportunities for improvement by regularly monitoring and assessing compliance and CSR performance. This involves monitoring stakeholder comments, CSR results, and compliance indicators.

Involving stakeholders in compliance and CSR initiatives promotes trust and addresses issues. Both projects are more successful when stakeholders are involved, and there is open communication between them.

There are various obstacles to overcome while juggling CSR with compliance. Allocating resources between compliance and CSR programs can provide issues for organizations. Careful planning and prioritization are necessary to guarantee both areas receive sufficient funding and assistance.

Objectives of CSR may occasionally clash with legal constraints. For instance, promoting ambitious environmental goals could oppose legal restrictions. Organizations need to resolve these disputes to take a well-rounded strategy.

Regulatory regulations can be complex, making matching CSR objectives with compliance difficult. Businesses need to be updated on legal developments so they may modify their procedures as required.

It might be challenging to gauge if CSR activities are performing and to report on compliance. For organizations to monitor their progress and inform stakeholders of their findings, they require efficient tools and procedures.

Several businesses have effectively combined compliance and CSR, showing how these ideas may complement one another to produce advantageous results.

Patagonia is renowned for its steadfast dedication to ecological sustainability. The business supports conservation initiatives and encourages responsible sourcing, abiding by the law, and adhering to environmental rules.

Through its Sustainable Living Plan, which has objectives about social responsibility, the environment, and moral business conduct, Unilever unifies CSR and compliance. The business ensures its CSR efforts comply with industry norms and legal regulations.

Microsoft prioritizes community involvement, environmental sustainability, and moral behavior in its corporate responsibility initiatives. The business pursues CSR objectives like philanthropy and carbon neutrality while upholding a strict compliance framework.

Organizations looking to accomplish regulatory compliance and positive social impact must balance compliance and corporate social responsibility. While CSR goes beyond legal requirements to address greater ethical and social duties, compliance offers the legislative framework for ethical company activities. Organizations may effectively manage both aspects by integrating compliance and CSR strategies, creating comprehensive policies, implementing governance structures, encouraging a culture of responsibility, and involving stakeholders. A company's reputation, risk management, and stakeholder trust are all improved by the effective integration of CSR and compliance despite obstacles, including resource allocation, competing goals, intricate legislation, and measurement hurdles. Ultimately, sustainable business practices and long-term performance are facilitated by a balanced approach to compliance and CSR.

Whistleblowing and Legal Protections

To keep accountability and integrity in businesses, whistleblowing is essential. It entails reporting wrongdoing, unlawful activity, or unethical behavior by personnel in an organization. Whistleblowers need the legal safeguards surrounding them to be encouraged to come out without fear of reprisals. This section examines the idea of whistleblowing's importance, and the legal safeguards that protect those who do it.

The act of revealing wrongdoing, whether it involves criminal activity, fraud, corruption, or transgressions of ethical standards, is referred to as whistleblowing. Employees, contractors, or anyone with direct knowledge of the wrongdoing can act as whistleblowers. Whistleblowing is frequently done primarily to protect moral principles, guarantee accountability, and avert harm.

They notify management or other specified internal authorities about wrongdoing within the company. With this strategy, businesses may deal with problems before they become more serious and involve outside parties.

Reporting wrongdoing to other parties, such as the media, law enforcement, or regulatory agencies, is known as "external whistleblowing." This action is usually taken when internal channels cannot resolve the problem, or the misconduct is highly visible to the general public.

Whistleblowing contributes to the accountability of organizations and the identification and prosecution of those who commit wrongdoing.

Whistleblowers shield the general public, customers, and other stakeholders from harm or exploitation by disclosing unlawful or unethical activity.

Whistleblowers encourage an ethical and transparent culture within their organizations by disclosing wrongdoing.

When spotting and dealing with regulatory infractions, whistleblowers are essential to overall legal compliance and enforcement.

Legal safeguards are intended to prevent retaliation against whistleblowers and guarantee that they can expose wrongdoing without suffering negative repercussions. Although these safeguards differ depending on the jurisdiction, they often consist of the following:

Legal safeguards shield informants against reprisals from employers or other company personnel. Termination, demotion, harassment, and discrimination are examples of retaliatory actions.

Whistleblower laws frequently contain clauses protecting the anonymity of those who come forward with misbehavior reports. Maintaining the integrity of the reporting process and preventing retaliation are two benefits of confidentiality.

When faced with retaliation, whistleblowers may be able to pursue legal action to obtain damages, reinstatement, and back pay, among other remedies. A method for resolving improper measures performed against whistleblowers is provided via legal remedies.

Several important laws and regulations protect whistleblowers—the United States Whistleblower Protection Act (WPA) of 1989. Federal workers who reveal information about unethical or criminal activity within their agencies are protected by this federal legislation. The WPA offers channels for reporting and addressing grievances and forbids retaliation against informants.

The United States' 2002 Sarbanes-Oxley Act (SOX). This statute safeguards employees of publicly traded corporations who come out with information about fraud or securities law infractions. Companies are required under SOX to set up processes for managing complaints from whistleblowers.

Dodd-Frank Wall Street Reform and Consumer Protection Act (Dodd-Frank) of 2010 (U.S.). Dodd-Frank creates a whistleblower program within the Securities and Exchange Commission (SEC) and strengthens whistleblower rights in the financial sector. It offers monetary rewards to those who disclose serious infractions.

The United Kingdom's Public Interest Disclosure Act (PIDA). This legislation protects employees who disclose malpractice or wrongdoing in the public interest. PIDA offers legal redress for unlawful dismissal and protects whistleblowers from reprisals.

The laws protecting whistleblowers (WPL) in different jurisdictions. Whistleblower protection laws are prevalent in many nations and offer protection and redress to those who expose wrongdoing. The scope and methods of enforcement of these laws differ.

Whistleblowers may encounter many obstacles despite legal safeguards. Notwithstanding their legal safeguards, whistleblowers could worry about reprisals from coworkers or employers. This kind of anxiety may prevent people from reporting wrongdoing.

Many potential informants need to be made aware of their rights or the safeguards that are in place for them. Insufficient knowledge may lead to an underreporting of wrongdoing.

Whistleblower protection litigation can be difficult and time-consuming to navigate. Legal support may be necessary for whistleblowers to pursue their claims successfully.

Whistleblower attitudes and organizational culture can affect how effective protections are. Whistleblowers may experience stigma or isolation in various settings.

There are various actions that organizations can take to support and foster whistleblowing. The reporting process is aided by establishing easily understandable ways for whistleblowers to report information. Both internal and external alternatives should be included in these processes.

Fostering an environment that values ethics and openness motivates staff members to voice their concerns. The leadership should support whistleblowers, and misbehavior should be quickly addressed.

Employees can become more aware of their rights and duties by participating in training programs on whistleblowing, legal protections, and ethical behavior.

Organizations must guarantee the protection of whistleblower identities and confidentiality during the reporting and investigation phases.

Whistleblowing is one of the most important tools for maintaining business responsibility and integrity. Whistleblower legal protections enable people to come forward with reports of wrongdoing without fear of reprisal. Despite obstacles and constraints, Whistleblower protections can be made more effective by integrating whistleblowing practices well, having transparent reporting procedures, and cultivating a positive workplace culture. Organizations may encourage whistleblowers, deal with misbehavior, and add to a climate of trust and accountability by creating an atmosphere that values openness and moral conduct.

Future-Proofing Your Compliance Program

Future-proofing a compliance program is crucial for firms hoping to succeed over the long run and negotiate a constantly changing regulatory environment. As rules and industry standards evolve, businesses must implement strategies that foresee future issues and meet existing compliance obligations. This section examines important tactics for ensuring a compliance program is future-proof, such as preemptive planning, technological integration, ongoing oversight, and cultivating a compliance culture.

The foundation of future-proofing a compliance program is proactive planning. Organizations must proactively predict and manage possible modifications to regulations and new hazards. Proactive planning's essential elements include:

Frequent risk assessments assist in locating possible vulnerabilities and dangers related to compliance. Organizations can create plans to reduce the risks associated with compliance by assessing both internal and external issues.

This entails imagining various future situations and evaluating how they might affect compliance. This aids businesses in getting ready for a range of legislative and sectoral changes.

Proactive planning requires staying current on impending industry trends and regulatory changes. Organizations can interact with legal and compliance experts, participate in industry forums, and subscribe to regulatory alerts to remain on top of developments.

Technology is essential to the modernization and long-term viability of compliance initiatives. Including cutting-edge technologies can improve productivity, precision, and flexibility. Principal domains of technology integration encompass.

Organizations can automate and streamline compliance operations by implementing complete compliance management systems. These systems can track compliance efforts, manage regulatory obligations, and produce reports.

Organizations can spot possible problems, track compliance performance, and discover patterns by utilizing data analytics. Data-driven decision-making can be supported, and compliance issues can be revealed with the help of advanced analytics.

By automating repetitive processes, evaluating massive volumes of data, and seeing patterns that can point to compliance problems, artificial intelligence (AI) and machine learning technologies help improve compliance. Future regulatory trends can also be predicted with the use of AI-powered solutions.

Including strong cybersecurity safeguards in the compliance program is crucial as data privacy and cybersecurity laws get stricter. This entails putting access limits, encryption, and frequent security assessments into place.

A compliance program must be continuously monitored and evaluated to be sure it stays relevant and successful over time.

Frequent internal audits assist in determining improvement areas and evaluating compliance systems' efficacy. Periodically scheduled audits covering different facets of the compliance program should be carried out.

Establishing and monitoring important compliance indicators enables firms to assess their performance and spot possible problems. Compliance rates, audit conclusions, and incident reports are a few examples of metrics.

Putting feedback tools in place, including stakeholder consultations and employee surveys, provides important insights into how well the compliance program is working—receipts aid in finding weaknesses and potential improvements.

Policies and procedures for compliance are kept current and useful by routinely evaluating and revising them. Companies need to be ready to modify their compliance program in reaction to new threats and changes in the law.

A robust compliance culture is necessary to guarantee compliance is incorporated into routine business operations. Developing a compliance culture entails:

An organization's dedication to compliance is reflected in its leadership. Senior management and executives should set an example for compliance by supporting initiatives.

Frequent training sessions aid staff members in comprehending regulatory requirements and their part in upholding compliance. Updates on regulatory changes should be included in training suited to certain roles.

It guarantees that workers understand their obligations when expectations and standards about compliance are communicated clearly. Employers should give staff members easy access to tools and channels so they may voice concerns and get advice.

Offering incentives and rewards to staff members who show a strong dedication to compliance promotes moral behavior and emphasizes the significance of compliance.

Interacting with stakeholders and experts from outside the program yields insightful information and helps future-proof the compliance process.

Using legal and compliance specialists enables firms to stay current on best practices and regulation changes.

Specialists can advise on difficult compliance matters and help formulate plans for upcoming difficulties.

Organizations can stay current on industry trends and regulatory developments by collaborating with peers in the sector and engaging in industry associations. Exchanges of best practices and solutions to shared problems can also arise from peer collaboration.

Businesses can better comprehend their needs and resolve their worries by interacting with stakeholders, such as clients, financiers, and authorities. Feedback from stakeholders can improve transparency and guide compliance measures.

Organizations must be on the lookout for new legislation and trends that may influence their operations to future-proof their compliance program.

The importance of ESG legislation is growing as stakeholders call for more responsibility and transparency. Companies need to get ready for the obligations of ESG compliance and reporting.

Regulations about data privacy, such as the California Consumer Privacy Act (CCPA) and the General Data Protection Regulation (GDPR), are changing quickly. Companies need to keep up with data protection regulations and take on new privacy-related issues.

Businesses have to manage a variety of regulatory standards across several jurisdictions as they operate in a global setting. It's critical to keep up with international regulations and modify compliance procedures as necessary.

The proactive and planned process of "future-proofing" a compliance program ensures businesses can handle new risks and regulation changes. Organizations can improve their compliance programs and achieve long-term success by putting proactive planning into practice, integrating cutting-edge technologies, monitoring and evaluating compliance regularly, cultivating a culture of compliance, interacting with external experts and stakeholders, and attending to emerging trends and regulations. In an ever-changing regulatory environment, a future-proofed compliance program supports organizational integrity, transparency, sustainability, and reducing risks.

CONCLUSION

The book "Mastering Regulatory Changes and Compliance: Strategies for Thriving in a Dynamic Legal Landscape" offers a thorough road map for navigating the complex and constantly evolving regulatory compliance landscape. It's important to consider the crucial realizations and tactics that will enable you to succeed in the face of regulatory complexity as we draw to a close on this journey.

Regulatory compliance is a strategic requirement for long-term corporate performance and a legal requirement. Create a solid compliance foundation that endures throughout time by comprehending the past and projecting future trends. It is impossible to overestimate the significance of industry-specific information, proactive response techniques, and ethical considerations. These components are the cornerstone of a successful compliance program, allowing you to control risks, stay out of trouble, and promote an ethical and responsible culture.

Throughout this book, we have stressed the requirement of adaptability and ongoing development in compliance practices. To keep your compliance program robust and active, it's imperative to invest in training, engage stakeholders, and leverage technology. When you put these techniques into practice in your business, the case studies and real-world examples given should be a great resource.

Ultimately, developing a forward-thinking, flexible organization that can confidently traverse the legal terrain is the key to conquering regulatory changes and compliance.

Thank you for buying and reading/ listening to our book. If you found this book useful/ helpful please take a few minutes and leave a review on the platform where you purchased our book. Your feedback matters greatly to us.

www.ingramcontent.com/pod-product-compliance
Lightning Source LLC
Chambersburg PA
CBHW072007150726
47999CB00002B/536